FINDING
the
AMERICAN DREAM

BILL CLEVLEN

Library of Congress Control Number: 2020938237

ISBN: 9781681062754

Cover design: Eric Marquard
Page design: Jill Halpin

Cover images: Eisenhower Home, Bill Clevlen; Ameria Earhart, Getty; Ruby slippers, Bill Clevlen; Mark Twain, public domain; Jim Henson and Kermit the Frog, Getty; Louis Armstrong, Library of Congress; Johnny Carson Home, Bill Clevlen.

All images by the author unless otherwise noted.

Printed in the United States of America
20 21 22 23 24   5 4 3 2 1

DEDICATION

This book is dedicated to Mac—
always dream big!

TABLE OF CONTENTS

Inventors & Founders

Historical Figures & Cultural Icons

Food & Drink

Humble Beginnings & Homes

INTRODUCTION

A few days before it opened to the public in 2014, I had the chance to visit the restored childhood home of Johnny Cash in rural northeast Arkansas. Cash grew up along a dusty gravel road surrounded by poverty, in a house provided by the US government shortly after the Depression. Driving away, I could barely see through the cloud of dust or handle the earsplitting sound the rough terrain was wreaking on my vehicle. As I made my way back to the main highway, I could finally hear some of my favorite Cash songs coming through the speakers. This was the moment I began to understand "the American dream."

As I've traveled around the country, I've been inspired by rags to riches stories that prove anyone in America can achieve greatness. Dreamers have come from every state, launching careers in smoke filled honky tonks, one-bedroom shacks, laboratories, cluttered garages, and yes, even along bumpy gravel roads in the middle of nowhere. Some sacrificed their lives, risked arrest, or faced impossible odds to achieve greatness.

The stories in this book will hopefully inspire you to work hard, focus on your own dreams, and know that anything is possible. And, it's never too late to get started! Did you know that Harland Sanders didn't begin work on Kentucky Fried Chicken until he was already in his 60s? Stan Lee didn't sell his first comic book until he was almost 40. Sam Walton was 44 when he founded Walmart.

Of course, this book isn't just about dreaming, it's also about travel. Each profile concludes with a specific location where you can personally connect with the legacies and achievements of these Americans that dared to dream. Add these great destinations to your future road trip plans and experience American history up close and in person.

MADE IN THE USA

ENTERTAINMENT

★ FINDING THE AMERICAN DREAM ★

Fred Rogers

A shy, introverted, and overweight boy would grow up to be the most beloved neighbor in television history.

It wasn't always a beautiful day in the neighborhood for Fred Rogers. He spent much of his childhood alone, and was often bullied at school for being overweight. Rogers learned to play piano at age five. As a teenager, he received his very own concert grand Steinway, a gift from his grandmother. It was the piano he would use for the rest of his life.

Fred believed television was a horrible influence on children and set out to change how the medium educated and shaped young minds. He began working with child psychologist Margaret McFarland to develop ideas for teaching children life lessons through storytelling.

After college, Fred spent more than a decade working various jobs in television. In 1968, *Mister Rogers' Neighborhood* launched on WQED TV in Pittsburgh. The show began to air regionally and then nationally on public television stations. Sensing the show's growing popularity, a Boston affiliate arranged a meet and greet for children to visit with Mr. Rogers. The staff prepared for as many as 500 attendees. More than 5,000 showed up.

Mr. Rogers truly cared about his young viewers and tackled important, relatable topics like war and divorce. He also helped ease the fears many children have, including obscure ones like being

TRIVIA

Q LONG BEFORE HE STARRED ON THE BIG SCREEN AS BATMAN, THIS HOLLYWOOD ACTOR WORKED AS A STAGEHAND ON *MISTER ROGERS NEIGHBORHOOD* AND CLAIMS FRED HAD A SLY, SNEAKY SENSE OF HUMOR.

Answer | **MICHAEL KEATON** |

HEINZ HISTORY CENTER IN PITTSBURGH, PENNSYLVANIA DISPLAYS SETS FROM *MISTER ROGERS' NEIGHBORHOOD.*

sucked down the drain in a bathtub.

He personally answered every piece of fan mail he received during his career, and the contents of those letters occasionally influenced the show. A young blind girl once wrote him and said she was afraid the fish were hungry since she couldn't see them being fed. After that, Rogers always announced when he was feeding the fish.

In 2003, Saint Vincent College launched the Fred Rogers Center in his hometown of Latrobe, about 40 miles east of Pittsburgh. Exhibits featuring Fred's original puppets, the Neighborhood Trolley, and Daniel Striped Tiger's Clock, are all on display and free to the public. In downtown Pittsburgh, the Heinz History Center maintains several set pieces from the show including King Friday's castle and the Great Oak Tree—home of the characters Henrietta Pussycat and X the Owl. Even the Pittsburgh airport gives visitors the chance to see personal items from Mr. Rogers—including his trademark blue shoes and red sweater.

There are two statues dedicated to Rogers around the region. One featuring Fred on a park bench in Latrobe, and the other located on the North Shore near Heinz Field.

THE FRED ROGERS CENTER
MONASTERY RD., LATROBE, PA 15650
FREDROGERSCENTER.ORG

HEINZ HISTORY CENTER
1212 SMALLMAN ST., PITTSBURGH, PA 15222
HEINZHISTORYCENTER.ORG

Dolly Parton

A poor girl from eastern Tennessee used writing, humor, and faith in God to ditch poverty and become America's sweetheart.

It's rare to find anyone these days that's universally loved as much as Dolly Parton. Her dream of stardom began early in life. Parton, along with her 11 siblings lived in a one-bedroom shack in eastern Tennessee. She's often described her family as "dirt poor." She shared a bed with sisters, and has noted that her father paid the doctor that delivered her with a bag of cornmeal.

After moving to Nashville, she earned success as a songwriter and in 1967 landed a spot on *The Porter Wagoner Show*. Later came a solo career with hit songs like "I Will Always Love You," considered by many to be the greatest love song of all time. By 1976, she had become a mainstream artist gaining traction on the pop charts and branching out beyond country music. Other hits included "Jolene," "9-5," and "Islands In the Stream," a duet with Kenny Rogers.

Dolly's sense of humor, with jokes mostly about herself, may be the legendary artist's most impressive talent. She earned a down-to-earth, approachable reputation by using lines like "it costs a lot of money to look this cheap." Or "I look just like the girls next door . . . if you happen to live next door to an amusement park."

Her own amusement park in Pigeon Forge is appropriately named Dollywood, and routinely ranks as the most visited tourist attraction in the entire state of Tennessee.

 DOLLY PARTON HAS DONATED OVER 100 MILLION OF THESE TO CHILDREN IN HONOR OF HER FATHER.

Answer **BOOKS**

THE CHASING RAINBOWS MUSEUM IS INCLUDED WITH AN ADMISSION TO THE DOLLYWOOD THEME PARK IN PIGEON FORGE. TENNESSEE.

The park is located near the Smoky Mountains, where Parton was raised. While visiting, guests can explore the Chasing Rainbows Museum which pays homage to Parton's incredible career. You'll see an endless amount of industry honors that include Grammys and statues from the Country Music Association, Academy of Country Music, American Music Awards, and People's Choice Awards.

The museum showcases items from Dolly's wardrobe, instruments, videos of interviews, and even one of a kind artifacts from Parton's life like love notes from her grade school days. You'll even see the childhood coat that inspired the song "Coat of Many Colors." Dolly wrote the song about a coat she wore, made from old rags that caused other children to laugh at her. The lyrics were scribbled down on the back of a dry cleaning receipt in 1969.

Don't forget to take a stroll through Dolly's tour bus which is parked on-site and see a replica of her childhood home. A statue of Dolly is located in nearby Sevierville.

DOLLYWOOD
700 DOLLYWOOD PARKS BLVD.. PIGEON FORGE. TN 37863
DOLLYWOOD.COM

DOLLY PARTON STATUE
125 COURT AVE.. SEVIERVILLE. TN 37862

Walt Disney

The magic all began under a cottonwood tree in small-town Missouri.

Walt Disney's biggest dreams began under a massive cottonwood tree on a 40-acre farm in Marceline, Missouri. The Disney family moved to the small town after leaving Chicago in 1906. Marceline would become the inspiration for many of the signature Disney characters and iconic sights like Disneyland's Main Street USA. Disney later returned to his childhood home in 1956. He spoke to adoring fans about his time in Marceline and how it had influenced his life. From beneath the shade of what he called The Dreaming Tree, a young Walt drew everything he saw from rabbits to field mice.

It is fitting that the Disney Hometown Museum is located in Marceline's former train depot because Walt and his brother would play near the tracks as children and soon developed a love for everything about trains. Exhibits inside the museum tell other stories of Walt's childhood and display personal artifacts like an honorary high school diploma he received in 1960. (He quit high school at age 16 to join the Red Cross Ambulance Corps during World War I.)

Visitors will likely hear about one life-changing moment Disney experienced during his childhood. Walt performed a "circus" with farm animals for kids in the neighborhood with a 10-cent admission. They enjoyed the first half but didn't like the second. Walt's mother insisted he refund his friends' money because they weren't "satisfied customers." A young Disney walked away from that experience with

 WHAT EARLY DISNEY FILM DID CRITICS SAY WOULD NEVER WORK, WITH SOME IN HOLLYWOOD LABELING IT "DISNEY'S FOLLY"?

Answer **SNOW WHITE**

THE WALT DISNEY HOMETOWN MUSEUM IS HOUSED IN THE 10,000-SQUARE-FOOT FORMER TRAIN DEPOT IN MARCELINE, MISSOURI.

a fresh outlook on the importance of good service. It's a lesson that is evident in how the Disney theme parks operate today—with lots of smiles and attention to detail.

Don't skip out on a slow drive by Disney's childhood home and be sure to take the short walk to a reproduction of the barn where Walt performed his circus act. The original Dreaming Tree is no longer standing but was replaced by a new tree, planted with soil from the Magic Kingdom. The excellent signage around town gives visitors a lot of great information and makes it simple to navigate all of the must-see spots.

Marceline is located along Missouri's Highway of the American Genius. The highway stretches from Hannibal to St. Joseph and features the hometowns of other American pioneers. Keep in mind, while the museum is typically open on Sundays, other businesses in town are usually closed.

WALT DISNEY HOMETOWN MUSEUM
120 E SANTA FE AVE., MARCELINE, MO 64658
WALTDISNEYMUSEUM.ORG

Johnny Cash

He went from living on a dusty gravel road in rural Arkansas to being one of the best-selling musicians of all time.

By the time Johnny Cash was five years old, he was already working in the cotton fields with his parents and singing songs about faith and God. His mother helped teach him to play guitar and by the age of 12, he was already writing songs.

He enlisted in the US Air Force in 1950 and worked as a Morse code operator. Four years later, he returned and settled in Memphis where he sold appliances while studying to be a radio announcer. At night he played in a trio known as The Tennessee Three and as a group, they would audition for legendary music producer Sam Phillips at Sun Studio.

Phillips had no interest in recording the gospel songs that Cash wanted to sing. It wasn't until the band discovered their rockabilly sound that Phillips took note and gave them their break. Cash went on to record some of the biggest country music titles of his generation and many of the songs are still popular today, hits like "Ring of Fire," "Folsom Prison Blues," and "I Walk the Line." Unfortunately, his success became overshadowed by excessive drug use and frequent run-ins with the law.

Many fans still think Cash spent time in prison but he never did, although his outlaw attitude along with the drugs and drinking had finally caught up with him by the late 1960s. With the help of relatives and singer June Carter, Johnny began to clean up his act

TRIVIA

Q NAME THE ACTRESS WHO PLAYED JUNE CARTER-CASH IN THE FILM *WALK THE LINE.*

Answer | **REESE WITHERSPOON**

LEFT: HAVING A SEAT IN JOHNNY'S FAVORITE CHAIR, A WORN-DOWN LEATHER RECLINER, INSIDE THE HIDEAWAY RANCH HOUSE IN BON AQUA, TENNESSEE. *RIGHT:* THE BED JOHNNY AND JUNE SLEPT IN THROUGHOUT THEIR ENTIRE MARRIAGE.

and regain his Christian faith. Once sober, Cash proposed to Carter while on stage in February of 1968. They were married a week later.

Cash died in 2003, less than four months after June.

Down a bumpy gravel road, a short drive from Memphis, you'll find the place where Cash was born and raised. The modest family home in Dyess, Arkansas, was built shortly after the Great Depression as part of President Franklin D. Roosevelt's New Deal. In fact, an entire colony of homes was constructed as an experimental program that gave away land and housing to farmers.

The home has always been a draw for longtime fans and tourists. However, until 2015, visitors left with an inaccurate impression of the Cash story. The house had fallen into disrepair and looked more like something in a ghost town than the home of a music legend. Arkansas State University decided to buy the property and refurbish it back to its original condition. Now guests can experience the home exactly as the Cash family did when they first moved in back in 1935.

Walking in the front door, you'll see the piano that Johnny's mother would play each night. There are two small bedrooms. When first built, the home did not have running water or electricity. In the colder weather, it was tough to keep warm. Yet, when they received it, the entire family sat on the floor of their brand-new home and cried—thankful to have it.

Two hundred and twenty miles to the east, the small town of Bon Aqua, Tennessee, offers another remarkable insight into the life of Johnny Cash. His ranch, known as Hideaway Farm, was a favorite getaway for the music legend who was recognized around the world. Cash called it "the center of my universe." This is where he filmed television shows and specials on a stage just yards from his house. You'll also see the "One Piece at a Time" car made famous from Cash's hit song in 1976.

The property is an incredible opportunity to see the relatively modest life that Johnny Cash lived despite his success. The two-story house was an hour away from his main residence in Hendersonville, Tennessee. (That property was destroyed in a fire in 2007.) You'll drive through security gates adorned with music notes after checking in at a former general store that now serves as a Johnny Cash museum. The most notable artifact inside is the large wooden bed that Johnny and June slept in for most of their marriage.

Another museum dedicated to the life and career of Johnny Cash is located in downtown Nashville. Nashville's Johnny Cash Museum features the largest and most comprehensive collection of Cash artifacts in the world.

Johnny and June were laid to rest in Hendersonville Memory Gardens a few miles northeast of Nashville.

JOHNNY CASH BOYHOOD HOME
110 CENTER DR., DYESS AR 72330
DYESSCASH.ASTATE.EDU

STORYTELLERS HIDEAWAY FARM
9676 OLD HWY. 46, BON AQUA TN 37025
STORYTELLERSHIDEAWAYFARM.COM

JOHNNY CASH MUSEUM
119 3RD AVE., NASHVILLE, TN 37201
JOHNNYCASHMUSEUM.COM

JOHNNY CASH'S BOYHOOD HOME IN DYESS, ARKANSAS.

Andy Griffith

A poor boy from the wrong side of the tracks helped introduce the world to Mayberry.

Andy Griffith was born and raised in a place he once described as "the wrong side of the tracks." As a baby, he slept in a dresser drawer since his parents couldn't afford to buy him a crib. Growing up, he was shy but discovered his sense of humor and used laughter to gain friends and his own identity. In high school, he developed a love of singing and even learned to play the trombone. He loved music and acting, taking an interest in school plays.

Griffith performed comic monologues on records in the 1950s and recorded Christian hymns and gospel songs over the years. He was raised Baptist and had entered college studying to be a pastor before changing his major to music and even teaching for a short time once he graduated from the University of North Carolina.

Andy Griffith spent decades as an actor in Hollywood, with many notable roles in film and television. His last steady role was as Detective Ben Matlock from 1986 to 1995. However, to most of his fans he'll always be remembered as Mayberry's common sense sheriff, Andy Taylor. Mayberry, the fictional hometown of Andy and his son Opie, was inspired by Griffith's real hometown, Mount Airy in North Carolina.

Mount Airy still represents the old-school, small-town charm that has always been synonymous with its fictional twin city. Mayberry isn't real, but walk past the Snappy Lunch diner or Floyd's Barber Shop on Main Street and you might think otherwise.

TRIVIA

 Q WHAT WAS THE NAME OF THE ICONIC WHISTLING THEME SONG THAT OPENED EACH EPISODE OF *THE ANDY GRIFFITH SHOW?*

Answer "THE FISHIN' HOLE"

THE MAYBERRY COURTHOUSE FEATURES SHERIFF ANDY TAYLOR'S DESK AND JAIL CELLS LIKE THE ONES FEATURED IN *THE ANDY GRIFFITH SHOW*.

Though the town of Mount Airy didn't really start to embrace Griffith's fame until the 1980s, today his legacy is on display all over the place. You can begin to explore the sites with a ride in one of the Mayberry squad cars starting at Wally's Service Station. The drivers will guide you around the area and point out must-see attractions including Griffith's childhood home.

Once you're back, walk next door to the replica Mayberry Courthouse. Step inside and discover a fun facsimile of the police station set from *The Andy Griffith Show*. You can sit behind Andy's desk, complete with the sheriff's nameplate and typewriter. Across the room, you can lock one of your relatives (or yourself) into a holding cell.

The Andy Griffith Museum is just a short drive away with the largest collection of memorabilia and artifacts related to Mount Airy's most famous resident. The exhibits include props and wardrobe pieces from *The Andy Griffith Show, Matlock*, and other notable television and film appearances.

Don't miss the beautiful statue out front that features Andy and Opie, both holding fishing poles. The statue was a gift from TV Land, the cable network known for playing classic American television programs.

Judy Garland

She went from the stage of a small-town theater in Minnesota to starring in the most popular film in American history.

Born in 1922, Frances Ethel Gumm would grow up to become one of the most celebrated and recognizable actors in the history of cinema. Gumm was raised in the small town of Grand Rapids, Minnesota, by parents who ran a local movie theater and performed vaudeville routines.

She was the youngest of three daughters who together formed a singing and dancing trio. The Gumm Sisters toured regularly and would change their name to The Garland Sisters shortly before they broke up in 1935.

Garland scored an audition with MGM studios and impressed the studio's co-founder Louis B. Mayer. While clearly a talent, her appearance was very different from that of many of the other leading female stars of the day. She was also incredibly small which proved to be challenging for studio producers; Garland stood a mere 4 foot, 11.5 inches.

Despite becoming a proven box-office draw for MGM, she was treated poorly by studio executives including Mayer who supposedly called her his "little hunchback." She was constantly forced to diet and was often only served soup and a plate of lettuce instead of regular meals.

In 1938, she was cast as Dorothy Gale in *The Wizard of Oz*. (Two other actors—Shirley Temple and Deanna Durbin—were both

Q IN THE BOOK VERSION OF *THE WIZARD OF OZ*, WHAT COLOR ARE DOROTHY'S SHOES?

Answer SILVER

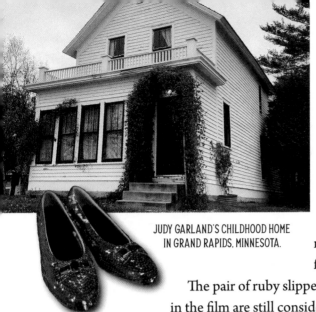

JUDY GARLAND'S CHILDHOOD HOME
IN GRAND RAPIDS, MINNESOTA.

offered the part before it was ultimately given to Garland.) *The Wizard of Oz* is considered the most widely viewed film in American history and has routinely been ranked one of the best films ever made.

The pair of ruby slippers that Garland wore in the film are still considered one of the most valuable pieces of film memorabilia. There are five known pairs of the shoes with one pair on display at the Smithsonian's American History Museum.

Garland went on to star in other films, including the 1944 hit *Meet Me in St. Louis* where she first introduced the world to a new song called "Have Yourself a Merry Little Christmas." In addition to films, she also hosted her own television program and performed in concert venues.

While living in London, Judy Garland was found dead at the age of 47 from an apparently accidental drug overdose.

Her Minnesota hometown of Grand Rapids preserved her childhood home which is part of a Judy Garland memorial and museum. It is known to include the world's largest collection of personal artifacts and *Wizard of Oz* collectibles. Exhibits include the carriage from the scene in the movie when Dorothy first arrives at the doors of Oz. The carriage was once owned by Abraham Lincoln.

JUDY GARLAND MUSEUM
2727 S POKEGAMA AVE., GRAND RAPIDS, MN 55744
JUDYGARLANDMUSEUM.COM

Elvis Presley

A C student in high school music class became the King of Rock and Roll.

Elvis Presley was born in 1935 and lived with his parents in Tupelo, Mississippi. The Presleys struggled financially and were evicted from their home not long after Elvis was born.

His first public appearance came in the first grade where he performed in a local talent show and finished in fifth place. A few months later, he received his first guitar, a birthday gift from his mother. He took lessons from family members and learned to play, though he was often too shy to sing in front of others. Growing up, Presley was regarded as a loner and teased as a "trashy" kid who liked hillbilly music. He would often bring his guitar to school and play during lunch.

In the fall of 1948, the family moved to Memphis and landed in a public housing complex. Elvis attended high school and received only a C in music class. His teacher told him he "didn't have any aptitude for singing."

In August of 1953, Presley visited Sun Records and made his first impression. Producer Sam Phillips noted that he was a "good ballad singer" but ultimately not the type of voice they were looking for. However, on July 5, 1954, almost one year later, his life would forever change.

Late in the evening during a subsequent visit to Sun Records, Elvis performed a song called "That's All Right, Mama." Phillips overheard

ELVIS PRESLEY'S CHILDHOOD HOME IN TUPELO, MISSISSIPPI.

4E 77
ELVIS AARON PRESLEY

Elvis Presley was born in Tupelo, Mississippi on January 8, 1935, the son of Vernon and Gladys Presley. He moved to Memphis in 1948. Soon after signing a contract with Sun Records in 1954 he achieved tremendous popularity. His musical and acting career in records, movies, television, and concerts made him one of the most successful and outstanding entertainers in the world. He died on August 16, 1977 and is buried here at his Memphis home, Graceland.

him singing from the control room and recorded what would be Presley's first single.

He would go on to record 18 No. 1 songs and sell more than one billion records worldwide. Interestingly, Elvis won only three Grammy awards and all of them were for gospel recordings. His star began to fade in the 1970s with a public divorce and substance abuse. Presley, who had become dependent on drugs and overweight, died in August of 1977.

Decades after his death, Presley's star remains profitable. *Forbes* magazine notes that he posthumously earned over $40 million in 2019 and is currently second on its top-earning, dead-celebrities list behind Michael Jackson.

Loyal fans can connect with the legacy of Elvis Presley at every phase of his life and career. The small two-room childhood home in Mississippi has been preserved along with the tiny church where he attended services with his family. Both are part of the Elvis Presley Birthplace Memorial in Tupelo. Visitors can pay to tour both buildings or see the exterior for free along with several statues.

Sun Studio, where Elvis was first discovered, is located in Memphis and open to the public. The tour includes a small museum with exhibits and collectibles that highlight the artists who made Sun Records famous. From there, visitors can walk down a short flight of steps and directly into the actual studio. Over the years, the studio itself hasn't changed. It still retains the same ceiling tiles and sound proofing along the walls that it did when artists like Elvis, Johnny Cash, Jerry Lee Lewis, and Roy Orbison recorded there.

Your tour will include a chance to hear some early Elvis recordings while you stand in the very spot where the future King of Rock and Roll laid down tracks.

Across town, Presley's Memphis home is one of the most-visited estates in America, second only to the White House. Graceland has been open to the public since 1982 and draws over 650,000 annual visitors. Inside the home, guests are allowed to see the living room, dining room, kitchen, game room, and the bedroom of Presley's mother.

There is also a TV room, the famous Jungle Room—complete with green shag carpet, a separate office space, and racquet ball court. Guests are not allowed on the top floor which includes Presley's bedroom where he died in 1977. His grave is located on the property as well.

Across the street from Graceland is a massive entertainment complex that features museums and restaurants along with both of Presley's personal airplanes. Visitors can see the jumpsuits worn in concerts, instruments, awards, paintings, records, and even a television that Elvis once shot with a gun.

In 2016, a new hotel complex called The Guest House at Graceland opened with 450 luxury guest rooms and dining options. Each evening, guests are treated to Elvis movies in a 464-seat theater, live music, and a nighttime peanut butter and banana sandwich buffet.

ELVIS PRESLEY BIRTHPLACE
306 ELVIS PRESLEY DR., TUPELO, MS 38801
ELVISPRESLEYBIRTHPLACE.COM

SUN STUDIO
706 UNION AVE., MEMPHIS, TN 38103
SUNSTUDIO.COM

GRACELAND
ELVIS PRESLEY BLVD., MEMPHIS, TN 38116
GRACELAND.COM

THE LIVING ROOM INSIDE GRACELAND, ELVIS PRESLEY'S MEMPHIS HOME.

Buddy Holly

A roller rink gig in Texas spawned a pioneer of modern-day popular music.

Buddy Holly lived a short life but achieved a lasting legacy as a music pioneer. Raised in the town of Lubbock, Texas, Holly developed an interest in country western and blue grass music. By age 15, he was performing around town at the local roller-skating rink, clubs, grocery store parking lots, and on KDAV, the town's radio station.

In 1955, an impressed talent scout arranged for Holly to sign a contract with Decca Records. He never connected with producer Owen Bradly, mostly because Holly had little control over his own music or recording sessions. He returned to Texas and learned of Norman Petty, an independent record producer about 100 miles west of Lubbock in Clovis, New Mexico.

It was in this small studio where Holly and his band The Crickets would find their unique sound and help transform popular music. The band would record 25 hit records by the time Holly turned 22 years old.

On February 3, 1959, Holly died in a plane crash along with musicians Ritchie Valens and The Big Bopper. The chartered aircraft went down in a frozen corn field in Clear Lake, Iowa, while headed to North Dakota. The event has become known as "the day the music died" thanks in part to a 1971 hit song by artist Don McLean called "American Pie."

In Lubbock, the Buddy Holly Center retains a collection of artifacts relating to his life. Fans can tour the house where he wrote many of his songs. The home he lived in when "That'll Be the Day"

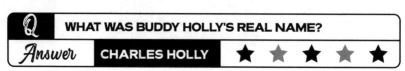

TRIVIA

Q WHAT WAS BUDDY HOLLY'S REAL NAME?

Answer CHARLES HOLLY ★ ★ ★ ★ ★

became a No. 1 song is still standing, though it is still a private residence. The city of Lubbock provides a map to all of the notable Holly sites around town.

Buddy Holly's legacy certainly extends beyond Texas. Fans can still visit the recording studio where

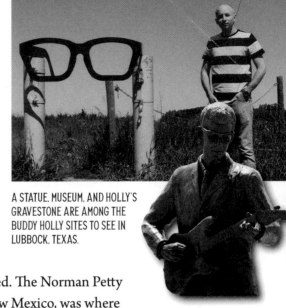

A STATUE, MUSEUM, AND HOLLY'S GRAVESTONE ARE AMONG THE BUDDY HOLLY SITES TO SEE IN LUBBOCK, TEXAS.

many of his songs were produced. The Norman Petty Recording Studio in Clovis, New Mexico, was where Holly returned after an unsuccessful stint in Nashville. The studio was used by other famous performers like Waylon Jennings and Roy Orbison.

The site of Holly's plane crash in 1959 is marked by a memorial and a large replica of his signature glasses. It's a short drive off the main highway while passing through Clear Lake, Iowa. His final resting place is in the City of Lubbock Cemetery where his headstone includes a guitar and reads: "In loving memory of our own Buddy Holly."

LUBBOCK, TEXAS SITES:
BUDDY HOLLY CENTER
1801 CRICKETS AVE.,
BUDDYHOLLYCENTER.ORG

BUDDY'S 1957 HOME
(PRIVATE RESIDENCE—
PLEASE BE RESPECTFUL.)
1305 37TH ST.

BUDDY HOLLY GRAVE SITE
31ST ST. & TEAK AVE.

OTHER NOTABLE LOCATIONS:
NORMAN PETTY
RECORDING STUDIO
1313 W 7TH ST., CLOVIS, NM 88101

PLANE CRASH SITE
315TH ST. & GULL AVE.
IN CLEAR LAKE, IA

Johnny Carson

A Midwestern boy turned a love of magic into a career as the most frequently viewed television personality in American history.

For 30 years, millions of Americans ended their day with Johnny Carson, host of NBC's *The Tonight Show*. His program kick-started the careers of countless comedians including stars like Jerry Seinfeld, David Letterman, and Ellen Degeneres.

Long before "Here's Johnny" became a familiar phrase to the entire country, a young Carson dabbled in other forms of entertainment. As a kid, he learned magic tricks and performed around town with a cape his mother made for him. After college, he worked in radio and local television. He was always humorous.

An early job involved working on a morning TV show where, among other things, he'd interview pigeons on the roof of the local courthouse and ask them about political corruption. Carson hosted other television programs including the show *Who Do You Trust?* where he met sidekick Ed McMahon.

Carson initially declined the offer to replace Jack Paar as host of *The Tonight Show*. He was eventually convinced and in 1962 began an unprecedented 30-year run as a late-night television host. Though his first year was rocky, he found his footing and enjoyed big ratings and big money.

His final show was in 1992 and unlike many celebrities who retire, he truly disappeared from the public eye. Carson, a longtime smoker, died from respiratory failure at the age of 79.

 Q IN 1973, STORE SHELVES WERE EMPTIED NATIONALLY AS CONSUMERS HOARDED THIS HOUSEHOLD PRODUCT AFTER CARSON JOKED THAT THERE WAS A SHORTAGE OF IT.

Answer **TOILET PAPER**

JOHNNY CARSON'S CHILDHOOD HOME IN CORNING, IOWA.

While Carson often spoke of his Nebraska roots, he was actually born in Iowa. The home he lived in is open for tours in the small town of Corning. You can see the room where Carson was born and experience the town he lived in until the age of eight.

His Nebraska roots run much deeper and the town of Norfolk has fully embraced his legacy. A large mural showing the progression of Carson's career is a fantastic spot to take a photo. You can also see the home that Carson lived in during his formative years. It's currently a private residence but a historic marker sits outside the house.

Carson was known to be generous to the town of Norfolk with millions of dollars in donations for community projects including a cancer center and an endowment of $33 million to his alma mater, the University of Nebraska. With part of that funding, the college opened the Johnny Carson School of Theater and Film.

At the Elkhorn Valley Museum, visitors will find a small exhibit of *Tonight Show* artifacts including Johnny's six Emmy awards. Other items include cue cards, the Art Fern costume, and his Presidential Medal of Freedom.

JOHNNY CARSON BIRTHPLACE
500 13TH ST., CORNING, IA 50841
JOHNNYCARSONBIRTHPLACE.ORG

ELKHORN VALLEY MUSEUM
515 QUEEN CITY, NORFOLK, NE 68701
ELKHORNVALLEYMUSEUM.ORG

Evel Knievel

An adventure-seeking boy from rural Montana grew up to become America's best-known daredevil.

America's most notable daredevil grew up in Butte, Montana, where he dropped out of high school to work in a copper mine. He was fired after doing wheelies on heavy duty equipment and crashing into the town's main power lines. That first public stunt left the entire town of Butte without electricity for several hours.

Whether it was ski jumping or rodeos, Knievel was always looking for a challenge. He joined the US Army in 1950 and qualified for its track team where he became a pole vaulter. After his time in the service, he returned to Montana and started a semi-professional hockey team. Other odd jobs along the way included selling insurance and working as a hunting guide.

He moved his family to Washington state in the 1960s and opened up a Honda motorcycle dealership. Looking for additional ways to provide for his family, he decided to produce a local stunt show. In his first performance, he jumped a motorcycle over a box of rattlesnakes and two mountain lions.

In the years ahead, Knievel experienced success as well as serious injuries stemming from these stunt shows. One early performance involved another moving motorcycle that resulted in a direct hit to his groin when he failed to jump fast enough. He began jumping over cars in 1966 with mixed results. A show in Missoula, Montana, landed him a broken arm and several cracked ribs. In 1967 after

TRIVIA

Q WHAT DID EVEL KNIEVEL DO TO MAKE SURE ACTOR GEORGE HAMILTON WOULD PORTRAY HIM RESPECTFULLY IN A 1971 FILM?

Answer HE HELD HIM AT GUNPOINT AND MADE HIM READ THE SCRIPT!

jumping 16 cars, he took a fall from his bike which resulted in a concussion. The same stunt a month later resulted in a broken wrist, knee, and two ribs.

His biggest jump, as well as his largest amount of national exposure up to that date, came from a horrifying crash in Las Vegas. On New Year's Eve 1967, Knievel jumped 141 feet, flying over the fountains at Caesars

THE EVEL KNIEVEL MUSEUM IN TOPEKA, KANSAS, INCLUDES COSTUMES, HELMETS, MOTORCYCLES, AND VEHICLES ALL USED DURING HIS CAREER.

Palace but ended on the pavement after missing the landing. He was rushed to the hospital and feared dead. He survived and—battered and bruised—Evel Knievel was now more famous than ever before.

In 1968, he returned to jumping and earned around $25,000 per appearance. The coming years resulted in more success and more crashes; becoming a superstar had taken a tremendous toll on his body. The *Guinness Book of World Records* claims that Knievel holds the title for the most bones ever broken with 433. However, in a 2014 interview his son claimed that the number was actually closer to 50.

The last major jump happened in 1977 when he lost control during a rehearsal in Chicago. Knievel was attempting to jump over a shark tank and crashed into a cameraman. Later that year, the TV sitcom *Happy Days* showed Henry Winkler as The Fonz attempting to jump over a shark tank, coining the phrase "jumping the shark."

Evel Knievel spent his final years helping to promote his son Robbie who continued the daredevil legacy. In 2007, Knievel died at the age of 69 after serious health setbacks including strokes due to his many head injuries.

The Evel Knievel Museum in Topeka, Kansas, is a well-designed tribute to every aspect of the daredevil's legacy and career. On display are some of Knievel's iconic jumpsuits that became a signature part of his stunts along with his helmets and motorcycles. Visitors may be surprised to see the hospital X-rays from various injuries resulting from crashes included in the exhibit.

Some of the most notable artifacts are the Evel Knievel toys and products. By 1972, he had started licensing his name and image to be placed on products and collectibles. There were very few things off limits and as a result the number of branded items is overwhelming.

Memorabilia include Evel Knievel lunch boxes, board games, and clothing. Toys and play sets like the Canyon Cycle or Scrambler Van are sure to ignite childhood memories for fans who watched Knievel in their youth. All of the action figures include a separate helmet as safety was always an important message conveyed during his public appearances and stunts.

The biggest draw to the museum is a 4-D virtual reality attraction where visitors can hop on a motorcycle and feel the thrill of jumping over 16 cars. A museum employee stands close by for safety to prevent guests from falling off the bike due to its incredibly legit, lifelike experience.

EVEL KNIEVEL MUSEUM
2047 SW TOPEKA BLVD., TOPEKA, KS 66612
EVELKNIEVELMUSEUM.COM

Louis Armstrong

A poor boy from New Orleans grew up to remind us that we live in a wonderful world.

Louis Armstrong was raised in a New Orleans neighborhood so rough it was known locally as the Battlefield. He quit school in the fifth grade so he could work full-time.

Armstrong was arrested at the age of 11 after shooting blanks from his father's gun to ring in New Year's Day 1913. He was sent to an all-boys reform school on the outskirts of the city. As fate would have it, this otherwise sobering experience would help set the stage for the rest of his life.

While serving more than a year in the Colored Waif's Home for Boys, Armstrong learned to properly play the cornet. Soon after his release, he became one of the most in-demand cornetists in the region. In 1922, Armstrong set his sights on Chicago where he joined his mentor, Joe "King" Oliver. By 1925, he was recording his own albums and playing with five—then seven—other musicians to create an all new jazz sound.

Armstrong invented his own style using improvised musical solos along with his unique vocals.

His sound remained popular enough to knock The Beatles from the top of the charts during the height of "Beatle mania" and well into the 1960s. His biggest hit, "Hello Dolly," remained on the Hot 100 chart for 22 weeks. He became the oldest person (at age 62) to score a chart-topping single in 1964. Amazingly, his most well-known song, "What a Wonderful World," was not a hit until 1987. It was recorded

Q WHAT DID ARMSTRONG HAND OUT AS GIFTS TO ADORING FANS AND ADMIRERS AFTER IT HELPED HIM LOSE WEIGHT IN THE EARLY 1950S?

Answer **AN HERBAL LAXATIVE CALLED SWISS KRISS**

ARMSTRONG'S HOME IN QUEENS, NEW YORK, HAS BEEN OPEN TO THE PUBLIC SINCE 2003. ARMSTRONG LIVED THERE FROM 1943-1971. THE MUSEUM DISPLAYS PERSONAL ARTIFACTS INCLUDING HIS TRUMPET.

four years before his death, but only after being featured on the soundtrack for *Good Morning, Vietnam* did it become popular.

His distinct sound lead to severe lip damage from the force used to hit the toughest notes. His nickname "Satchmo" stems from the size of his mouth. One childhood nickname was "Satchel Mouth" which was incorrectly used by a British magazine editor who called Armstrong "Satchmo."

The Louis Armstrong House in Queens, New York, features artifacts from various collections relating to the historic musician. You'll see items like his gold-plated trumpet, clothing, photos, and manuscripts. Armstrong's personal collection included 86 scrapbooks, 5 trumpets, 14 mouthpieces, 120 awards, and 650 home-recorded reel-to-reel tapes. He lived in the house from 1943 to 1971.

Armstrong's birthplace in New Orleans was demolished in 1964, but a historical marker marks the spot where his childhood home once stood.

LOUIS ARMSTRONG HOUSE MUSEUM
34-56 107TH ST., QUEENS, NY 11368
LOUISARMSTRONGHOUSE.ORG

John Wayne

A boy from Iowa grew up to be a symbol of patriotism and American pride.

Marion Robert Morrison was born in 1907 in the town of Winterset, Iowa. He grew up in Southern California and began to work in the film industry as a prop man, extra, and bit actor. His first starring role was in 1930 for the film *The Big Trail*. His screen name, John Wayne, was invented by director Raoul Walsh and Fox executive Windfield Shehann, although Wayne retained his real-life childhood nickname of "Duke" throughout his career.

Throughout the 1930s, John Wayne became a talented actor while working on Western feature films and serials. He developed his own style of walking, talking, and acting on screen by spending considerable time with real-life cowboys. Wayne became a serious actor in the 1940s and worked his way up to becoming a household name. He appeared in more than 160 feature films including *Stagecoach, The Shootist, Red River, The Alamo, The Longest Day, How the West Was Won*, and *The Man Who Shot Liberty Valance*. However, his only Academy Award win came for his leading role in the film *True Grit*.

Wayne was not only a movie star but he became an important figure in American culture. His name and image still evoke patriotism and American exceptionalism. He toured regularly to entertain troops with the USO.

A heavy smoker, Wayne began battling cancer in 1964 and lost his left lung and several ribs. He held a press conference in his living room

TRIVIA

Q JOHN WAYNE WAS KNOWN TO LOVE WHAT BOARD GAME?

Answer CHESS. HE PLAYED IT OFTEN WITH CELEBRITIES OF HIS DAY INCLUDING ROCK HUDSON. MARLENE DIETRICH. AND ROBERT MITCHUM.

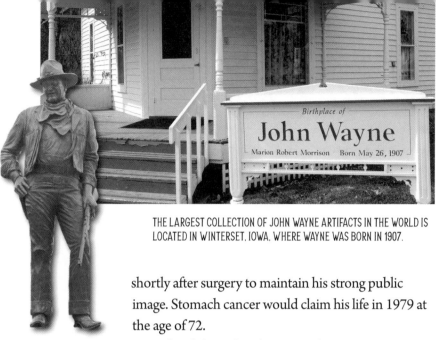

THE LARGEST COLLECTION OF JOHN WAYNE ARTIFACTS IN THE WORLD IS LOCATED IN WINTERSET, IOWA, WHERE WAYNE WAS BORN IN 1907.

shortly after surgery to maintain his strong public image. Stomach cancer would claim his life in 1979 at the age of 72.

His family's modest four-room home in Winterset, Iowa, has been restored to reflect its appearance in 1907, the year of the actor's birth. The John Wayne Birthplace Museum sits adjacent to the home and is the place where fans can view the largest collection of John Wayne artifacts in existence. Exhibits include original movie posters, film wardrobe, scripts, contracts, letters, artwork, and sculptures. A highlight of the collection is one of Wayne's last customized automobiles and an eye patch he wore in the 1969 film *True Grit*.

Visitors can also have a seat in the museum's cozy movie theater and view a documentary on the Duke's film career. The theater seats were once used in the historic Grauman's Chinese Theater in Hollywood.

Be sure to explore the beautiful town of Winterset and the rest of Madison County, Iowa. The area was featured in the classic film *Bridges of Madison County*. The covered bridges, still intact, are a major draw for tourists.

JOHN WAYNE BIRTHPLACE MUSEUM
205 S JOHN WAYNE DR., WINTERSET, IA 50273
JOHNWAYNEBIRTHPLACE.MUSEUM

Patsy Cline

Despite a rough and prematurely shortened life, she managed to become one of America's most memorable singers.

Patsy Cline was born and raised in Virginia. The modest two-story home in Winchester where she lived from ages 16 to 21 is now a tourist attraction. Cline suffered many personal setbacks in her life: She was abused by her father as a child, she was hospitalized for rheumatic fever at age 13, and later in her life, she suffered from chronic headaches and back pain as a result of a car crash in 1961.

Patsy taught herself to play piano as a young child but didn't have an interest in singing until she was 16. Cline began singing on local radio shows and competing in singing contests. She scored her first recording contract in 1954 but failed to gain much traction. It wasn't until 1957, when she appeared on *Arthur Godfrey's Talent Scouts* and performed a song called "Walking After Midnight" that she skyrocketed to the top of the country music charts.

In the 1960s, Cline joined the Grand Ole Opry and found success with hit songs like "He's Got You," "Back in Baby's Arms," "Leavin' on Your Mind," and "Sweet Dreams." Then, during the height of her career, she died in a tragic plane crash on March 3, 1963. Cline was only 30 years old.

The crash site, deep in the woods of Camden, Tennessee, is marked by a large boulder. The inscription notes the names of all who died and reads: "Lost Their Lives in a Plane Crash." At the end

TRIVIA

Q WHAT PROLIFIC SONGWRITER AND COUNTRY MUSIC SINGER WROTE "CRAZY," PATSY CLINE'S BIGGEST HIT SONG?

Answer **WILLIE NELSON**

THE PATSY CLINE MUSEUM IS LOCATED DIRECTLY ABOVE THE JOHNNY CASH MUSEUM IN DOWNTOWN NASHVILLE, TENNESSEE.

of the long pathway down to the site of the crash, there is also a small gazebo and a historic marker.

In 2017, a Patsy Cline Museum opened in downtown Nashville. (It is located upstairs from the Johnny Cash Museum on Third Avenue South.) The museum has a small but impressive collection of Cline artifacts, most of which came directly from Charlie Dick, Patsy's husband. Charlie died in 2015 and left a treasure trove of personal effects including Patsy's wedding album, boot-shaped lighter, and handwritten letters from fans. Other items on display include Cline's awards, her Jimmy Dean Fan Club membership card, and wardrobe pieces used in concerts. You'll also see the Elgin watch she was wearing at the time of her death. The watch was a gift from her husband.

A jukebox in the museum plays two of Cline's songs that made it on the list of the Top 20 Jukebox Hits of All Time. The songs are "Crazy" (1) and "I Fall to Pieces" (17).

PATSY CLINE MUSEUM
119 THIRD AVE. S.
NASHVILLE, TN 37201
PATSYMUSEUM.COM

PATSY CLINE PLANE CRASH SITE
2904 MT. CARMEL RD..
CAMDEN, TN 38320

PATSY CLINE'S VIRGINIA HOME
608 S KENT ST., WINCHESTER, VA 22601

Prince

A musical genius from Minneapolis sells over 100 million albums worldwide.

Prince was born and raised in Minneapolis, Minnesota. By the age of 7, he had mastered the piano and by 14, he could play guitar and drums. His career achievements include over 100 million albums sold, over 40 hit songs with five reaching the top of the charts. It's estimated that Prince wrote as many as 1,000 songs during his career.

He is best known for songs like "Little Red Corvette," "Purple Rain," "When Doves Cry," "1999," and "Kiss." In 2007, Prince performed during the halftime show at Super Bowl XLI. It was viewed in over 140 million households and in 2015 was called "the greatest Super Bowl performance ever" by *Billboard Magazine*. He was inducted into the Rock and Roll Hall of Fame in 2004.

In 1987, Prince opened a 65,000-square-foot complex called Paisley Park near Minneapolis. It included a residence, recording studios, night club, event space, and business offices. The concept was to have every part of the creative process under one roof. At Paisley Park, Prince could record songs, film movies or music videos, play instruments, throw parties, or just relax. It was considered the first of its kind in the music business. Prince made it clear that after his death, he wanted Paisley Park to be open to the public. He was found dead inside one of the building's elevators in 2016 after an apparent overdose of fentanyl. Tours of the complex began not long after.

While hardcore fans may appreciate it more than others, it's still an interesting look behind the scenes of such an influential musician

Q	WHY DID PRINCE START USING A SYMBOL IN PLACE OF HIS REAL NAME IN 1993?	
Answer	HE WAS UNHAPPY WITH HIS RECORD CONTRACT WITH WARNER BROTHERS.	★

PAISLEY PARK WAS THE CREATIVE AND ENTERTAINMENT COMPLEX FOR LEGENDARY MUSICIAN, PRINCE. IT IS LOCATED NEAR MINNEAPOLIS AND OPEN FOR TOURS.

and producer. The general tour includes a look at the main floor and studios where Prince recorded some of his biggest hit songs. You'll also see the soundstage and concert hall where Prince rehearsed for tours and held private events and concerts. Fans can see his kitchen, piano room, and private night club. All tours get to see artifacts from Prince's personal archives including his wardrobe, awards, instruments, artwork, and motorcycles. Visitors are not allowed to see his private residence.

There are two other options that offer longer tours and more experiences. The most expensive option lets you record a song in one of Prince's recording studios. All tours have a strict photo policy and you'll be required to place your phones or smart watches in a special locked carrying case until the end of your visit.

PAISLEY PARK
7801 AUDUBON RD., CHANHASSEN, MN 55317
PAISLEYPARK.COM

Jimmy Stewart

By all accounts, this native of Indiana, Pennsylvania truly had a wonderful life.

Jimmy Stewart was born and raised in eastern Pennsylvania. He attended Princeton University where he first became interested in acting. After college, Stewart took on roles in various theater productions where he often received positive reviews. His first on-screen appearance was in the 1934 comedy short *Art Trouble*. Later that year, Stewart signed a seven-year contract with MGM though the movie studio did not initially see him as a leading man.

During his career, Jimmy Stewart appeared in more than 90 films and television shows. His most notable films included *Mr. Smith Goes to Washington*, *The Philadelphia Story*, *Harvey*, *Rear Window*, *The Naked Spur*, and *Anatomy of a Murderer*.

Stewart was the first major movie star to enlist in the United States Army in World War II. He was initially turned down because he didn't weigh enough. During his service, he appeared in a documentary called *Winning Your Wings* which was shown in movie theaters in 1942. It resulted in 150,000 new Army recruits.

His first film after the war was *It's a Wonderful Life*. The 1946 Christmas drama received a lukewarm response from audiences and did not become recognized as a holiday classic until the 1980s. Stewart plays George Bailey who is magically shown by an angel what the world would be like if he had never been born. The American Film Institute has called it one of "the best 100 American

TRIVIA

Q WHAT 1981 FILM DID JIMMY STEWART TURN DOWN? HINT: ITS LEAD ROLE INSTEAD WENT TO HENRY FONDA AND EARNED 10 OSCAR NOMINATIONS.

Answer **ON GOLDEN POND** ★ ★ ★ ★ ★

films ever made." Stewart called it the favorite film of his career.

The Jimmy Stewart Museum is located in Stewart's hometown of Indiana, Pennsylvania. The exhibits showcase his work in radio, film, and television. You'll also learn about his life in the military and as a family man. You can view film clips in a vintage 1930s movie theater, complete with velvet drapes and wine-colored seats. The projection system was donated by Universal Studios in Hollywood.

A STATUE OF JIMMY STEWART WAS UNVEILED ON HIS 75TH BIRTHDAY IN HIS HOMETOWN OF INDIANA, PENNSYLVANIA.

Other items on display include movie posters, awards, and mementos personally selected by Stewart. Those one-of-a-kind objects include a Winchester commemorative rifle and a propeller blade autographed by the cast of *Flight of the Phoenix*.

There's also a museum dedicated to the film *It's a Wonderful Life* in upstate New York. Many believe the town of Seneca Falls was the inspiration for Bedford Falls in the now-classic holiday film. Frank Capra visited the town while he was writing the screenplay and there are many similarities that have led even former members of the cast to make the connection.

JIMMY STEWART MUSEUM
835 PHILADELPHIA ST.,
INDIANA, PA 15701
JIMMY.ORG

IT'S A WONDERFUL LIFE MUSEUM
32 FALL ST., SENECA FALLS, NY 13148
WONDERFULLIFEMUSEUM.COM

Lucille Ball

They told her she'd never make it. She did. And she was hilarious.

Lucille Ball was born and raised in the town of Jamestown, New York. In her younger days, she worked as a model and attended drama school. Her instructors insisted she had no future in the entertainment industry.

After years of small movie roles in Hollywood and appearances on Broadway, Ball appeared on a radio program called *My Favorite Husband*. The show was a hit and was later developed for television. Lucy insisted that CBS hire her husband of 10 years, Desi Arnaz, to play the role of Ricky Ricardo. The network initially refused, saying audiences would never accept a Cuban married to an American girl. CBS folded after Lucy threatened to walk away if Desi wasn't hired. The result made *I Love Lucy* one of the most beloved television series of all time. It was the most popular show in America for four of its six seasons.

Ball became a pioneer in television as the first to use a studio audience with multiple cameras and sets adjacent to one another. It was also the first scripted television show to be shot on 35mm film. Her work as an actress and producer earned her recognition of all types. She graced the cover of *TV Guide* a record 39 times and was awarded two stars on the Hollywood Walk of Fame in addition to numerous awards.

TRIVIA

Q LUCY AUDITIONED FOR A LEAD ROLE IN WHAT AWARD-WINNING 1939 FILM? HINT: SHE DIDN'T GET THE JOB WHICH INSTEAD WENT TO VIVIEN LEIGH.

Answer **GONE WITH THE WIND**

LEFT: NEW YORK. THE DESILU MUSEUM FEATURES SETS FROM THE SHOW INCLUDING THE RICARDO'S LIVING ROOM. *RIGHT:* A MURAL CELEBRATING *I LOVE LUCY* IN JAMESTOWN.

Her production company, Desilu, produced several popular television programs including *The Untouchables, Mission: Impossible,* and *Star Trek.* It was sold in 1967 to Paramount Pictures.

Though famous for her red hair, Lucy was actually a natural brunette. She began to dye her hair in the early 1950s at the urging of executives at MGM.

Each year, fans from all over the world visit the Lucille Ball Desi Arnaz Museum in Jamestown. The facility is split into sections highlighting the couple's careers and personal lives, along with the production of *I Love Lucy.* Visitors will see what was once called the most famous living room in television history where, upon entering, Ricky Ricardo would announce, "Lucy, I'm home!" Another set piece highlights a favorite episode where Lucy is a spokesperson for a product called Vitameatavegamin. In the episode, Lucy drinks so much of the product that she becomes intoxicated while filming the commercial. There is also a life-size mural of the show's original studio audience.

While visiting Jamestown, you can also drive by Lucy's childhood home and pay your respects at her final resting place at Lakeview Cemetery.

LUCILLE BALL DESI ARNAZ MUSEUM
2 W 3RD ST., JAMESTOWN, NY 14701
LUCY-DESI.COM

Tina Turner

A stage in a one-room schoolhouse in Tennessee led to the rise of the undisputed Queen of Rock and Roll.

Tina Turner was raised in the town of Nutbush, Tennessee. Growing up, she often sang in school and during church services at the local Spring Hill Baptist Church. Her parents had a toxic relationship which eventually led Turner and both of her sisters to live with their grandmother. As a high school student, she was both a cheerleader and a basketball player.

At age 16 she moved to St. Louis, Missouri. After graduation, she became a nurse's aide at a local hospital. In her free time, she frequented local night clubs in the region and met Ike Turner who had a band called Kings of Rhythm. Once they began performing together, they started the Ike & Tina Turner Revue.

While her birthname was Anna Mae Bullock, Ike created the stage name Tina Turner. He went as far as copyrighting the name once they formed a duo: that way if she ever left him, he could legally replace her with another Tina Turner. Ike was the leader, but Tina was front and center during their performances and together they became one of the hottest acts of the early 1960s.

Their first single together, "A Fool in Love," was an instant hit reaching No. 2 on the R&B music chart. By 1966, Tina Turner was recording solo records and achieving success with songs like "River Deep-Mountain High." Ike and Tina would join The Rolling Stones on tour and reach a new level of stardom with appearances on programs like *The Ed Sullivan Show* and *American Bandstand*. In

TRIVIA

True or False? TINA TURNER HAD HER LEGS INSURED FOR $3.2 MILLION.

Answer TRUE ★ ★ ★ ★ ★ ★ ★ ★

THE SCHOOLHOUSE WHERE TURNER ATTENDED GRADE SCHOOL IS NOW A MUSEUM IN BROWNSVILLE, TENNESSEE.

1971, they achieved their biggest hit song, a remake of Creedence Clearwater Revival's "Proud Mary." The duo split in 1976 largely due to Ike's addiction to drugs.

After a few years of playing smaller venues, and being viewed mostly as a former star, Turner released the album Private Dancer. It was her fifth solo album, but its huge success launched her as a formidable solo performer. A *Los Angeles Times* music critic noted, "Her voice melts vinyl."

The 1980s made Tina Turner a superstar with hit songs like "What's Love Got to Do with It," "Better Be Good to Me," and "The Best." By the 1990s, she had been inducted into the Rock and Roll Hall of Fame, received a star on the Hollywood Walk of Fame, and earned countless industry awards.

In 2000, her Twenty Four Seven concert tour grossed $100 million and was the biggest tour of the year. She announced her retirement at its conclusion but would appear again nine years later for another tour to celebrate her 50th anniversary in the music business. It would go on to be one of the most successful tours of all time.

Turner officially retired in 2009 and became a citizen of Switzerland. In 2018, she revealed that she had suffered a stroke.

In an interview with Oprah Winfrey, she recalled being told that she wouldn't be able to walk again. Turner said she yelled, "Bull crap!" and then hit the floor as she tried to get out of bed. She went on to say that afterwards she became determined to overcome the setback and eventually taught herself to walk again.

In her memoir titled *My Love Story*, she also shared that she had received a kidney transplant from her husband Erwin Bach.

The school that Turner attended in the 1940s is now a museum dedicated to her life story and career. The one-room building where she studied until the eighth grade is known as the Flagg Grove School and is now part of the West Tennessee Delta Heritage Center. In 2012, the schoolhouse was dismantled and moved from its original location. Having fallen into disrepair, the school was rebuilt piece by piece, replacing each of the worn-out boards. Locals raised more than $150,000 to bring the building back to life and create the Tina Turner museum.

Turner herself donated many of the items on display. Some of the exhibits include the outfit she wore on the 50th anniversary of the Grammys, a fan letter from Prince Charles, and her yearbook from Sumner High School in St. Louis, Missouri. The stage in that school was where Tina would often perform along with her classmates.

Admission to the museum is free. A special Tina Turner Days celebration happens there each fall.

TINA TURNER MUSEUM
FLAGG GROVE SCHOOLHOUSE
121 SUNNY HILL COVE, BROWNSVILLE, TN 38012
WESTTNHERITAGE.COM

Jim Henson

A boy from rural Mississippi would bring fictitious characters to life and forever change the art of puppetry.

Jim Henson grew up in Leland, Mississippi, a small town not far from the border of Arkansas. He moved with his family to University Park, Maryland, in the late 1940s. The biggest event of his childhood was the arrival of a television into their home.

He began creating puppets at a young age. In high school, his characters were used on a local weekend television program. As a freshman in college, he created *Sam and Friends*, a five-minute children's show for WRC-TV. While working there, Henson produced a prototype for a new character called Kermit the Frog.

Henson explored changing how puppet characters were captured on camera. He began using metal rods to control their arms and used his own hand to make the mouth move. He also insisted that puppeteers use their own voices which helped make the characters come to life.

He worked in television—mostly in commercials—after graduating college. That led to talk show appearances featuring his puppets which included Rowlf, a piano-playing dog. By the late 1960s, Henson had been approached to create a children's program called *Sesame Street.* That program gave birth to characters like Big Bird, Ernie, Bert, Elmo, Cookie Monster, Count von Count, and Oscar the Grouch.

By 1976, Henson had developed a television program for an adult audience. All of the major American networks rejected it. An entertainment investor named Lew Grade saw the potential and

Q IN ADDITION TO THEIR CREATOR, JIM HENSON, WHICH TWO MUPPETS HAVE STARS ON THE HOLLYWOOD WALK OF FAME?

Answer KERMIT THE FROG, BIG BIRD

THE CENTER FOR PUPPETRY ARTS IN ATLANTA, GEORGIA, ROTATES MORE THAN 500 ARTIFACTS IN THEIR PERMANENT JIM HENSON GALLERY.

financed a syndicated version in England called *The Muppet Show.*

Henson had success with other television projects like *Fraggle Rock* and feature films like *The Muppet Movie.* His creative expertise was often sought for outside projects; for example, George Lucas hired him to help with early *Star Wars* films.

In 1990, Henson died from bacterial pneumonia at the age of 53. According to his will, no one in attendance at his funeral was allowed to wear black.

In 2015, the Center for Puppetry Arts in Atlanta received an incredible donation from the family of Jim Henson. Over 500 artifacts, including original Muppet characters are now part of the museum's permanent collection. Every six months, a rotating batch of Henson creations are available to view up close in their Jim Henson Collection.

Curators with the museum say that people have been known to cry when they see the real Muppets up close. It's a special childhood link for most visitors.

The Henson family also donated Jim's workspace—including a desk and other Muppet workshop tables and gadgets used while he was alive. Looking at the creative process is just as fun as seeing the final products. Henson would use all sorts of odd things to create the perfect puppets. Visitors can actually touch and feel random objects and materials that go into designing the characters. Fans of *Fraggle Rock, Dark Crystal,* and

other Henson productions won't be disappointed—you'll find characters from those series as well.

The Henson family has always had a close connection to the Center, which serves mostly as an educational facility. The huge collection required some adjustments, including an expanded storage facility to house all of the characters and other items.

The most common phrase heard about the Henson collection? "Big Bird is such a big bird!" Sounds hilarious but people are apparently stunned at just how big he is in person. (In case you're wondering, his exact height is 8 feet, 2 inches, and about 4,000 feathers.)

Henson's legacy has been preserved in other museums as well. In Leland, Mississippi, a gift from Jane Henson is on display at the town's visitor center. Known as the Birthplace of the Frog, fans can learn about Jim's childhood and the place where Kermit was envisioned.

At the Museum of the Moving Image in New York City, another permanent gallery dedicated to Henson gets visitors up close to nearly 50 original Henson characters. The Muppets on display include the Swedish Chef, Miss Piggy, and the heckling duo of Statler & Waldorf. The gallery also features material from Henson's experimental film projects and early creative work.

An original Kermit the Frog is also part of the Smithsonian's American History Museum and periodically on display to the public.

CENTER FOR PUPPETRY ARTS
1404 SPRING ST.,
ATLANTA, GA 30309
PUPPET.ORG

LELAND MS VISITOR CENTER
415 S DEER CREEK DR., LELAND,
MS 38756
BIRTHPLACEOFTHEFROG.ORG

MUSEUM OF THE MOVING IMAGE
3601 35TH AVE., ASTORIA, NY 11106
MOVINGIMAGE.US

George Jones

He grew up listening to the Grand Ole Opry and died the King of Country Music.

George Jones was born and raised in southeast Texas. Life was off to a rough start the moment he was born in 1931; a doctor dropped baby Jones and broke his arm. As a child, his father was physically and mentally abusive to Jones and his siblings. His father would occasionally return home after a night of drinking with friends and demand young George sing for them or else he would receive a beating.

Good memories from childhood included listening to the Grand Ole Opry on Saturday nights. His favorite performers on the show were Roy Acuff and Bill Monroe. However, the singer who influenced Jones the most as a child was Hank Williams.

In the mid 1950s, he landed the nickname "The Possum" while working at a local radio station. One of the deejays noted that Jones's facial features, including his short haircut, resembled the look of a possum. That moniker would stick with him his entire life.

His singing career began in 1954 and scored modest success—even a couple top-10 hits. But in 1959 when Jones recorded a song called "White Lightning," his music career finally took off. Later in life, Jones admitted that it took him more than 80 times to record the vocals for that song because he was so drunk.

His drinking continued but so did a string of hit songs over the next 20 years. Songs like "The Race Is On," "She Thinks I Still Care," "A Picture of Me (without You)," "The Grand Tour," and "A Good Year for the Roses" were among the dozens of hit songs Jones recorded.

Q WHO DID JONES SAY WAS HIS FAVORITE COUNTRY SINGER OF ALL-TIME?

Answer   MERLE HAGGARD   ★ ★ ★ ★ ★

GEORGE JONES ONCE DROVE HIS TRACTOR TO A BAR IN TOWN AFTER HIS CAR KEYS HAD BEEN TAKEN AWAY.

The most notable story about Jones and his drinking revolves around a riding lawnmower that he once drove to a bar after his car keys had been taken away. The lawnmower is on display at the George Jones Museum in Nashville. However, despite all his achievements, alcohol and drug abuse took a toll on his body and Jones was admitted to rehab in 1967.

George was married four times during his life. His third wife was country music legend Tammy Wynette. The duo toured together and recorded several big hits, but "Mr. & Mrs. Country Music" eventually divorced in 1976.

Jones continued his drinking and drug abuse and had spiraled out of control by the late '70s. He lost everything, was homeless, and lived out of his car. His weight had dropped below 100 pounds. Still performing, he was notoriously late or absent so often that he earned the nickname "No-show Jones."

His life started to bounce back in 1980 when Jones recorded the song that would define his career. It's been called the saddest song ever recorded, and *Rolling Stone* named "He Stopped Loving Her Today" No. 4 on their list of the 100 Best Country Songs of All Time. Jones would earn a total of 16 more top-10 hits over that decade.

In March of 1984, he was mostly sober thanks in large part to his fourth wife, Nancy, who helped him clean up his act and kept him

THE ROOFTOP VIEW AT THE GEORGE JONES MUSEUM OFFERS ONE OF THE BEST VIEWS OF THE CUMBERLAND RIVER IN DOWNTOWN NASHVILLE.

away from drug dealers. He began to make up shows that he had skipped out on and started to turn his life around. However, Jones was involved in a much-publicized car accident in 1999 due to his driving drunk. Jones claimed in interviews that the crash was a turning point and that he told God "no more smoking and no more drinking."

In all, George Jones earned 69 top-10 singles during his career and was inducted into the Country Music Hall of Fame. He was named a Kennedy Center honoree in 2008.

Jones died in 2013 after living longer than many had ever anticipated, considering his troubled past. His funeral was held at the Grand Ole Opry in Nashville and was attended by family, friends, and many of the country music artists who considered him the greatest of all time.

Two years after his death, the George Jones Museum opened in downtown Nashville. His widow, Nancy, donated most of the belongings and artifacts relating to his music career. The result is one of the most comprehensive museums ever constructed for a musician. His entire life story is told through photos, instruments, awards, clothing, and even personal items like his license and Costco membership card. Listening stations allow visitors to sample many of his songs.

The museum's top-floor bar provides great views of the Cumberland River.

GEORGE JONES MUSEUM
128 2ND AVE., NASHVILLE, TN 37201
GEORGEJONES.COM

John Ringling

A son of German immigrants built an empire by creating the modern-day circus.

John Ringling was one of seven sons and a daughter born to German immigrants in McGregor, Iowa. He would become the best known of the five Ringling brothers who owned and operated America's most successful traveling circus.

In 1907, Ringling Bros. purchased Barnum and Bailey's Greatest Show on Earth. It continued to operate separately. But by 1918, the death of several brothers, a worldwide flu epidemic, and rising costs forced John to merge both operations into a mega circus. The show ran for 110 years until closing in 2017.

At its peak, The Greatest Show on Earth was employing over 1,100 workers. There were two circus troups that traveled in separate trains, each with about 60 train cars. The shows would alternate routes to bring fresh performances to the cities they toured. By 1950, everything was consolidated into one large train. Locals who couldn't afford a ticket to the show could still watch the parade of animals and performers who traveled from the train tracks to the performing grounds.

The circus was known for its elephants and other stunt-performing animals. Equally as amusing to the public were the sideshow acts. The circus featured oddities like bearded ladies or a man with no arms or legs they called The Human Snake. The man slithered about like a snake and would wow audiences by rolling his own cigarettes using only his mouth. Despite the obvious exploitation of the

TRIVIA

Q — WHAT IS THE NAME OF THE CIRCUS-THEMED FILM FROM 2017 THAT FEATURES ACTOR HUGH JACKMAN?

Answer — **THE GREATEST SHOWMAN**

THE RINGLING FEATURES A 44,000-PIECE MINIATURE CIRCUS LAYOUT THAT INCLUDES MOVING PIECES, A TRAIN, AND 7,000 FOLDING CHAIRS.

sideshow performers, the circus provided them with employment they wouldn't have had otherwise.

John Ringling became one of the wealthiest men in America. He invested in real estate, trains, and oil. However, the Great Depression caused him to lose nearly everything. Near the end of his life, a combination of bad investments, tax liens, and failing health left Ringling with about $300 in his savings account. John was the only Ringling brother who lived into his 70s; he was 71 when he died in 1936. His 66-acre property in Sarasota, Florida, was willed to the state upon his death.

Today, The Ringling is one of Sarasota's most popular tourist attractions. The property includes public park space, museums, and gardens. Ca' D'Zan, the 55-room mansion where the Ringling family vacationed during the winter months is also open for tours. You'll see first-hand what life was like for one of America's wealthiest families in the early 1900s. The home was built to exact specifications laid out by the Ringlings who brought most of their ideas back from Europe.

After touring the first floor of the mansion, visitors can hang out on the large patio where fancy yachts once docked and wealthy friends partied on the banks of the Sarasota Bay.

The Ringling property includes Bayfront Gardens with walking trails and Mable Ringling's rose garden. There are two large

museums: The State Art Museum of Florida and the Circus Museum. The art museum began from John Ringling's large personal collection of fine art and was donated to the state of Florida upon his death in 1936.

The Circus Museum is a must-see, even for those of us who were never crazy about the circus. It's absolutely fascinating to learn the history and see the intricate details of each part of the massive operation. Artifacts on display include props, wardrobes, parade wagons, and canons that once launched performers across the big top. The museum has a vast collection of advertising, promotional posters, and news stories from as early as 1816.

Of all the exhibits to see, the most impressive may be the 3,800-square-foot miniature circus display. The Howard Bros. Circus, built by designer Howard Tibbals, has 44,000 individual pieces built in 1/16th scale. Tibbals started building the display in 1956 and finally displayed it at the World's Fair in 1982. It includes a working train and many moving parts. Hand-carved details like 1,500 workers, 500 animals, 152 wagons and 7,000 folding chairs all make this the world's largest circus model and one of the coolest displays you'll ever see.

Be sure not to miss the Wisconsin train car used by John and Mable Ringling to travel across the country. You can poke your head inside to see luxuries—like a bathtub—that were simply not found on train cars at the time.

John and Mable are both laid to rest just steps away from the family mansion in the Secret Garden.

THE RINGLING
5401 BAY SHORE DR., SARASOTA, FL 34243
RINGLING.ORG

Berry Gordy, Jr.

An $800 loan from reluctant family members helped launch one of the most notable record labels in American history.

Neither Berry Gordy nor Motown was an overnight success. Gordy was born and raised in Detroit where he was the seventh of eight children. He dropped out of high school to become a boxer and spent time in the military after being drafted for the Korean War in 1952. Upon his return a year later, he developed an interest in writing songs.

Gordy worked for his father on the assembly line at the Ford Motor Company. To help pass the time and relieve the boredom, he wrote songs in his head. Some of those songs were recorded by local singers, one of which was a hit called "Lonely Teardrops," recorded by Jackie Wilson. Once Gordy studied his royalty checks, he realized that he needed to own his songs instead of just writing them for others.

After modest success as a songwriter, he dove into the world of producing and started building a lineup of local talent. His first big discovery was a group called The Miracles—led by a singer named Smokey Robinson.

Gordy's family loaned him a total of $800 to help start his own R&B record company. He purchased a home at 2648 West Grand Boulevard in Detroit for his base of operation which would later be called Hitsville U.S.A. Gordy and his wife lived upstairs with the lower level used for office space and a recording studio. During the peak Motown years, the doors to Studio A were open 24 hours a day, 7 days a week. Gordy understood that creativity doesn't always happen during

 WITH 12 NO. 1 SINGLES, WHAT WAS MOTOWN'S MOST SUCCESSFUL GROUP?

Answer **THE SUPREMES**

HISTORICAL STUDIO A IS ON THE LOWER LEVEL OF HITSVILLE U.S.A.. MOTOWN'S HEADQUARTERS IN DETROIT UNTIL 1968.

normal business hours. Even if a group decided at 3 a.m. they had a hit song to sing, they knew they had a place to record it.

While they didn't know it at the time, the halls of Hitsville U.S.A. were full of young performers who would go on to leave lasting impressions on the entire world. Stevie Wonder, Diana Ross, Michael Jackson, Gladys Knight, Marvin Gaye, and so many others created the unmistakable Motown sound. Groups like The Four Tops, The Marvelettes, The Supremes, Martha & The Vandellas, and The Temptations were making hit songs that have stood the test of time.

Gordy encouraged his lineup of talent and producers to compete for songs. Only after serious discussion and intense deliberation was a new song released to the public. Over the years, that formula churned out 191 chart-topping tunes like "My Girl," "Stop in the Name of Love," "I Just Called to Say I Love You," "Dancing in the Street," "How Sweet It Is," and "Please Mr. Postman."

Not only did Gordy have a formula for hit songs, he also worked to groom each Motown artist to thrive in public. The singers took classes from Maxine Powell, a former modeling school operator, who taught everything from public speaking to manners. Everyone took dance lessons from Cholly Atkins, a famous dancer from the 1930s. As polished as they appeared on stage, it's hard to believe that many of the Motown stars did not know how to move. Atkins taught groups

HISTORICAL STUDIO A IS ON THE LOWER LEVEL OF HITSVILLE U.S.A., MOTOWN'S HEADQUARTERS IN DETROIT UNTIL 1968.

like The Temptations and Four Tops simple steps that gave them the appearance of well-trained, in-sync dancers.

Standing inside Motown's historic Studio A, you can't miss the grand piano that's been heard on more hit songs than you can begin to count. (After touring the Motown premises, Paul McCartney paid to have the entire instrument refurbished and brought back to its former glory.) Up a few steps, behind a small window is the control room where sounds were mixed during recordings. Near the front door sits a small desk where Martha Reeves once answered phones as a receptionist before landing a contract of her own.

At the end of the hallway, you'll see a small vending machine where Stevie Wonder routinely grabbed one of his favorite candy bars–the Baby Ruth. It was common knowledge that the middle slot was reserved for Stevie so he could easily find it.

While upstairs, visitors can see the space where Gordy lived and check out a museum full of Motown artifacts including one of Michael Jackson's famous gloves. You'll also see an example of the echo chamber that producers used to add their distinct Motown sound to many of the recordings. The Motown Museum announced plans for a massive new addition in 2020.

MOTOWN STUDIO
2648 W. GRAND BLVD., DETROIT, MI 48208
MOTOWNMUSEUM.ORG

Walter Cronkite

A college dropout works hard to become the most trusted man in America.

Walter Cronkite was born in the town of St. Joseph near Kansas City, Missouri. At age 10, he moved with his family to Houston, Texas. In high school, he developed an interest in journalism while editing the school's newspaper.

Cronkite dropped out of college during his junior year at the University of Texas to focus on his love of journalism. His early resume included stints as a radio announcer, a sports columnist, and an overseas correspondent during World War II.

He was one of eight journalists selected to accompany the US Air Force during bombing raids over Germany. His coverage also included Germany's surprise 1944 attack on allied troops now known as the Battle of the Bulge.

By 1950, Cronkite was back working in the United States and part of the new CBS News television division. His first job was to anchor a 15-minute newscast on Sunday evenings called *Up to the Minute*. Over the next decade, Cronkite would produce documentaries, cover political news, and even host a news-themed game show.

In 1962, he took the reins of the *CBS Evening News* where he hosted a new 30-minute program highlighting the biggest stories of the day. The show was the first long-form nightly news program of its kind on television.

During Cronkite's tenure at CBS News he covered some of the biggest stories in modern American history, many of them while live

TRIVIA

 **WHAT LINE DID CRONKITE DELIVER AT THE END OF HIS NIGHTLY NEWSCASTS?**

Answer **"AND THAT'S THE WAY IT IS"**

THE WALTER CRONKITE MEMORIAL AT MISSOURI WESTERN STATE UNIVERSITY INCLUDES AN EXACT REPLICA OF HIS CBS NEWS STUDIO.

on the air. He narrated the video of NASA astronauts landing on the moon in 1969. "My palms are sweaty," he noted on camera as he waited for Apollo 11 to launch into space.

He would cover major events like the raucous 1968 Democratic convention, the Vietnam War, and Nixon's Watergate scandal. However, his most memorable on-air moment was in 1963 when he announced to the nation that President John F. Kennedy had been assassinated in Dallas, Texas.

Cronkite interrupted a soap opera to report on the event though there was no camera available in the news studio. With nothing more than the words "CBS News Bulletin" on screen, the audience could only hear the anchorman's voice sharing the brief details about the shooting. Shortly after, with another break in programming, Cronkite appeared on camera and would eventually deliver the news that Kennedy was in fact dead and Lyndon Johnson had been sworn in as the new president.

While Ed Sullivan generally earns credit for introducing The Beatles to the American public, it was in fact Cronkite who first told their story. The foursome was featured in a four-minute segment during the November 22, 1963, edition of the *CBS News*.

His unique delivery and trustworthy style earned him high marks with the general public. He had trained himself to speak slower than the average person so viewers could clearly understand him.

THE MEMORIAL ALSO INCLUDES A BRONZE BUST OF CRONKITE.

He spoke 124 words per minute, about 50 words per minute slower than the average American at the time. Perhaps this is part of why he became known as "the most trusted man in America."

Cronkite held the anchor chair at CBS until 1981. Following his retirement, he remained active as a journalist and television producer. He lived in New York City with Betsy, his wife of 65 years. Cronkite was an avid sailor and even learned to play the drums in his later years. He passed away in 2009. He was 92.

Missouri Western State University in St. Joseph opened the Walter Cronkite Memorial in 2013. The 6,000-square-foot facility located in Cronkite's hometown features a replica anchor desk with television cameras. Visitors can sit behind the desk, next to a typewriter and old-school telephone and pose for a picture. A replica pair of eyeglasses that Cronkite was known to wear are also available to help you play the part.

The school's collection of artifacts includes personal items like a signed photo from President Ronald Reagan, eight of Cronkite's Emmy awards, and the actual office desk he used while at CBS News. Other display cases highlight Cronkite's love of space exploration and his beloved wife.

A large mural displays various moments of his long career in news broadcasting while a remarkably accurate bronze bust of Cronkite sits atop a granite pedestal. A kiosk in the museum shows continuous footage from notable broadcasts.

WALTER CRONKITE MEMORIAL
MISSOURI WESTERN STATE UNIVERSITY
4525 DOWNS DR., ST. JOSEPH, MO 64507
WCM.MISSOURIWESTERN.EDU

MADE IN THE USA

INVENTORS
& FOUNDERS

★ FINDING THE AMERICAN DREAM ★

Thomas Edison

A "difficult" student becomes one of the most brilliant inventors of all time.

Thomas Edison was born in Milan, Ohio, in 1847. Early struggles in life included hearing loss and being labeled a "difficult" student by his grade-school teacher. His mother, a teacher herself, decided to homeschool Edison. By the time he was 15, Edison was working as a traveling telegrapher and filling in for workers who had left to fight in the Civil War.

At 21, he was living in Boston and working for Western Union. In his spare time, Edison invented an electronic voting recorder which would be the first of his many patents. The machine would allow voters to press "yes" or "no" instead of having to write their choices down on paper.

Over the years, Edison would change the world with his original inventions and improvements to existing technology. His most notable work dealt with the light bulb although many mistakenly believe that Edison was its inventor. Seventy-six years before Edison began his work on perfecting the light bulb, Humphry Davy introduced the first electric lamp. However, it was not a practical invention as the light was too bright and it didn't last long. Edison's improvements set the stage for production of a practical incandescent lamp, with light bulbs becoming commercially available starting in 1880.

Thomas Edison is known as one of the greatest inventors in American history. During the course of his life he received 1,093

A STATUE OF EDISON OUTSIDE THE MENLO PARK LABORATORY AT THE HENRY FORD MUSEUM.

US patents. He invented the phonograph, a device that would record sound. The first words he said into the device's microphone were, "Mary had a little lamb." His invention allowed troops in World War I to listen to music which brought Edison worldwide fame. Other notable inventions included the modern-day electrical grid, motion pictures, fuel cell technology, and alkaline batteries.

Edison's experimental laboratory in West Orange, New Jersey, has been preserved and is open for self-guided tours throughout the year. Visitors can explore 20,000 square feet of exhibit space and two floors of the main laboratory which was once closed to the general public. The facility first opened in 1876 to house Edison's expanding operations. His home, known as the Glenmont Estate, is also open for tours. The 29-room Victorian mansion is where the Edisons lived while raising their three children.

The family spent most winters at their estate in Fort Myers, Florida, along the Caloosahatchee River. It has been open to the public since 1947. Henry Ford, a longtime friend of Edison, purchased a winter home on the same property which is also open for tours.

THOMAS EDISON
NATIONAL HISTORICAL PARK
211 MAIN ST., WEST ORANGE, NJ
07052
NPS.GOV/EDIS

EDISON FORD WINTER ESTATES
2350 MCGREGOR BLVD.,
FORT MYERS, FL 33901
EDISONFORDWINTERESTATES.ORG

THOMAS EDISON BIRTHPLACE MUSEUM
9 N EDISON DR., MILAN, OH 44846
TOMEDISON.ORG

John Deere

A Green Mountain boy rose from young blacksmith to America's agricultural hero.

In 1804, John Deere was born and raised in Rutland, Vermont. He learned the trade of blacksmithing at age 17. He'd later relocate to Grand Detour, Illinois, where he would invent a brand-new type of plow. By 1841, Deere was producing 100 plows annually. The company headquarters moved to Moline, Illinois as demand increased. By 1857, John Deere was producing more than 10,000 plows. In 2013, *Smithsonian* magazine named Deere's plow as one of the "101 Objects That Made America." The plow was chosen to become one of 137 million artifacts in their collection.

Deere & Company has continued as a viable family-run company through five generations. When farm equipment became motorized, the company expanded its production to include a larger variety of agricultural equipment under the leadership of Charles Deere.

Deere was 82 years old when he died in 1886, nearly three decades before his name became synonymous with the tractor business. It's hard to believe that he was never able to see his name on one of those iconic green machines.

The John Deere Company has preserved its historical sites and invites the public to tour them for free. The John Deere Pavilion in Moline, Illinois, gives visitors the opportunity to climb into the cab of some of the company's biggest machines. You'll learn about combines, dozers, excavators, and other tools used in farming. See how they operate, how they're built, and how they make a huge difference

TRIVIA

Q DEERE & COMPANY WORLD HEADQUARTERS WAS DESIGNED BY A FINNISH-AMERICAN ARCHITECT NAMED EERO SAARINEN. WHAT IS EERO SAARINEN MOST FAMOUS FOR DESIGNING?

Answer THE GATEWAY ARCH IN ST. LOUIS

THE JOHN DEERE PAVILION IN MOLINE, ILLINOIS, IS ONE OF MANY JOHN DEERE TOURIST ATTRACTIONS IN THE QUAD CITIES REGION.

on farms, big and small, all around the world. There are interactive exhibits as well as videos that share the vision of John Deere. Next door to the Pavilion is a large gift shop with hundreds of items bearing the company name and logo.

The John Deere Tractor & Engine Museum gives visitors an up-close look at the John Deere collection of equipment. It's located at the site of the very first John Deere factory in Waterloo, Iowa. You'll see how John Deere used his skills as a blacksmith to change farming. Interactive exhibits include testing your strength with a steel plow.

John Deere's former home is another site that's open for tours. You are welcome to explore the rooms of the home to see how they spent their free time. You can also stand in the very spot where he created the first commercially successful steel plow. On-site you'll find excavated artifacts and hear recordings of Deere himself as he describes how he built his business.

The company's headquarters and manufacturing sites also offer public tours. There are five plants that produce everything from tractor cabs to engines. The full list of tour times and directions are available on the company website.

JOHN DEERE PAVILION
1400 RIVER DR.,
MOLINE, IL 61265

JOHN DEERE HISTORIC SITE
8334 S CLINTON ST.,
GRAND DETOUR, IL 61021

JOHN DEERE TRACTOR & ENGINE MUSEUM
500 WESTFIELD AVE., WATERLOO, IA 50701
DEERE.COM

Harley & Davidson

Determined and innovative, two childhood friends create the largest motorcycle company in the world.

Bill Harley and Arthur Davidson were both born and raised in Milwaukee, Wisconsin. They were friends as well as neighbors living just a few doors apart on Ninth Street. As a teenager, Harley became interested in bicycles, the popular new form of transportation at the time. At age 15, he started working at a local bicycle shop. He'd later work as a draftsman at an electrical motor shop. Arthur Davidson worked at the same shop as a patternmaker. At the age of 21, Bill Harley developed plans for his first attempt at building a motor-bicycle. Bill and Arthur were eventually joined by two other Davidson brothers—Walter and William.

Harley-Davidson began producing motorcycles in 1903 in a 10 foot-by-15 foot wooden shed. Early bikes were used mostly for racing. As the years continued, their company continued to grow, and their products continued to be more advanced. By 1920, Harley-Davidson was the largest motorcycle company in the world. As of 2020, there are more than 1,500 dealerships in North America, South America, Asia, and Europe. Per capita, South Dakota has the most Harley-Davidson motorcycle owners of any state in the United States.

The Harley-Davidson Museum is one of Milwaukee's most popular tourist attractions. It's located just a few miles from where the company began and where its international headquarters are still located. The majority of visitors to the museum are not Harley riders. Anyone can

TRIVIA

Q WHAT MIDWEST CITY PURCHASED THE FIRST HARLEY-DAVIDSON MOTORCYCLE FOR ITS POLICE DEPARTMENT IN 1909?

Answer **DETROIT**

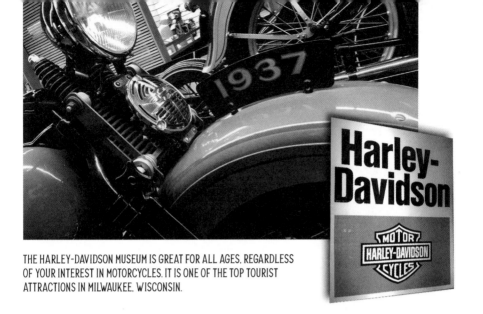

THE HARLEY-DAVIDSON MUSEUM IS GREAT FOR ALL AGES, REGARDLESS OF YOUR INTEREST IN MOTORCYCLES. IT IS ONE OF THE TOP TOURIST ATTRACTIONS IN MILWAUKEE, WISCONSIN.

enjoy the exhibits and fascinating story behind Harley-Davidson, regardless of whether you know anything about motorcycles.

The museum complex occupies 20 acres along the Milwaukee riverfront. You'll see more than 450 bikes dating back to Serial Number One, the oldest known Harley-Davidson motorcycle. The Experience Gallery lets you climb onto one of about a dozen various Harley models and watch a video about the great roads of America. You can also experience a virtual motorcycle ride using the museum's JumpstartTM demo, all while safely situated on a secure platform.

Also, be sure to check out Harley-Davidson's first "headquarters." A replica of the tiny shed that was first used to produce motorcycles sits near the front of the museum campus. After your tour, the Harley-Davidson gift shop has everything you could possibly imagine with the company logo attached, and the MOTOR Bar & Restaurant is located on the campus for a quick bite to eat. Free parking is available on the street in front of the museum and in the Parking Gardens across from the museum via Canal Street.

HARLEY-DAVIDSON MUSEUM
400 W CANAL ST., MILWAUKEE, WI 53201
H-DMUSEUM.COM

J.C. Penney

A Missouri man proved that a combination of vision, hard work, and strong ethics can equal big success.

J.C. Penney has been a mainstay of department store shopping in America for decades. Its founder, James Cash Penny of Hamilton, Missouri, was born in 1875. He was the seventh of twelve children and one of six who made it to adulthood. After high school, he began working for a local retail store. He never attended college.

In 1898, Penney was diagnosed as being susceptible to tuberculosis. He moved out West for a drier climate and began working for the Golden Rule dry goods stores in Denver. His work ethic impressed the owners who offered him a share in the company and the chance to open his own location in Wyoming. Eventually, Penney bought out all three of the store locations and planned on opening more.

Penney was a religious man who believed in honesty and hard work. As he opened new stores, his associates were trained to find similar workers who shared the same ethics and high standards. By 1912, Penney had opened 34 Golden Rule stores and moved his headquarters to New York. A year later, the stores changed names and became part of the new J.C. Penney Company.

In 1924, J.C. Penney opened the 500th store location in his hometown of Hamilton. Riding high with more than 1,000 locations across the country in 1928, financial ruin was right around the corner. J.C. Penney became a publicly traded company one week

TRIVIA

Q J.C. PENNEY ONCE EMPLOYED THIS YOUNG MAN AS MANAGEMENT TRAINEE IN DES MOINES, IOWA. HINT: HE'D GO ON TO BECOME ONE OF THE WEALTHIEST BUSINESS OWNERS IN THE WORLD.

Answer SAM WALTON OF WALMART

LEFT: THE J.C. PENNEY BOYHOOD HOME IN HAMILTON, MISSOURI. *RIGHT:* J.C. PENNEY'S OFFICE DESK INSIDE THE J.C. PENNEY MUSEUM.

prior to the historic 1929 stock market crash. Penney lost most of his wealth and had to borrow against life insurance policies to keep the company afloat.

Penney served on the company's board of directors until 1946 and continued to work in his office until he died in 1971. As of 2020, there were 875 J.C. Penney locations remaining nationwide.

His legacy is honored in Missouri along the state's Way of the American Genius. US Route 36 includes the childhood hometowns of Penney, Walt Disney, Mark Twain, Walter Cronkite, and other famous Missourians. The city of Hamilton has restored the house where Penney grew up and maintains a small library and museum downtown. The museum includes Penney's office desk and other rare artifacts relating to his life and career.

The very first J.C. Penney location, located in Kemmerer, Wyoming is still open for business. Down the street you'll find Penney's small, family home still intact and open to the public for tours. He lived there from 1904–1909.

J.C. PENNEY MUSEUM & BOYHOOD HOME
312 N DAVIS ST.
HAMILTON, MO 64644
CITYOFHAMILTON.COM

J.C. PENNEY STORE #1
722 J.C. PENNEY DR.
KEMMERER, WY 83101

Jenny Doan

She shared her knowledge with complete strangers and became the most famous quilter in the world.

Jenny Doan learned to sew when she was 10 years old. She began sewing costumes for a local theater group in California where she lived with her husband and children. With the rising costs of living out West and financial troubles after her youngest son developed a tumor on his lymph gland, they decided to leave. Doan looked at a map of the United States and randomly placed her finger on a spot in the Midwest. It turned out to be the town of Hamilton, Missouri.

After relocating and settling her family into the tiny town of 1,500 she started taking a class on how to quilt. Her new hobby would soon become a business. After learning she had to wait longer than a year for a local shop to finish one of her quilts, her family encouraged her to open a business of her own. In 2008, in a small brick building in downtown Hamilton, Doan opened the Missouri Star Quilting Company. She worked at the shop with her two daughters, while her two sons helped her launch an online store.

YouTube was already a powerful tool for many industries and interests long before Doan got involved. Colorful personalities had already carved a niche for themselves sharing tips on topics like car repairs, cooking, building furniture, or gardening. One popular topic that lacked high-quality videos and relatable tutors was quilting. Doan's son suggested that she record a couple tutorials to post on the platform. Doan responded: "Sure. What's a tutorial?" Today, her channel has the largest following in the world of quilting and receives millions of views annually.

TRIVIA

Q WHERE IS THE NATIONAL QUILT MUSEUM LOCATED?

Answer PADUCAH, KENTUCKY ★ ★ ★ ★ ★

THE SMALL TOWN OF HAMILTON, MISSOURI, HAS BEEN TRANSFORMED INTO A THRIVING COMMUNITY THANKS TO DOAN'S QUILTING BUSINESS.

Her instructional videos aim to keep quilting simple and fun. She's connected with viewers all over the world, with many of them adding a trip to Hamilton to their bucket lists. Over the years, new quilting shops have sprung up in town as well as restaurants and venues for retreats and classes. Thanks to Doan and her family, Hamilton has transformed from a sleepy small town to a destination with renewed interest and life.

For quilt lovers or travelers who enjoy seeing small towns roar back to life, Hamilton is worth the road trip. While you're in town, see the childhood home of another famous entrepreneur, J.C. Penney. The town is located along Missouri's Way of the American Genius which highlights famous Americans from St. Joseph to Hannibal.

VISITHAMILTONMO.COM

Joyce Hall

A boy from Nebraska overcame poverty and turned his passion for creativity into a new industry and a billion-dollar brand.

Joyce Hall was born in 1891 and raised in Nebraska. As a young man, Hall teamed up with his two brothers to open a postcard business but it didn't last for long. At age 18, Hall dropped out of high school and took his postcards to Kansas City, Missouri. He sold them to local drug stores and gift shops. After a fire in 1915 wiped out his inventory, he began to create original cards.

Imagine creating a new product and sending it to stores that didn't order it, along with a bill for the merchandise. That's pretty much what J.C. Hall did, sending packets of 100 greeting cards to various dealers throughout the Midwest. Some returned the cards with angry notes, others kept them and never paid. However, one third of the recipients responded by sending a check to the young entrepreneur in Kansas City, Missouri. The gamble earned Hall $200 which kickstarted the company that would eventually be known as Hallmark. Against the advice of others, he started advertising. The decision made Hallmark the most recognizable brand in the industry.

While greeting cards were typically sent for just Christmas and Valentine's Day, Hall banked on the idea that consumers could also be persuaded to send cards for birthdays and other casual occasions. He was right. By 1920, the roaring success of Hallmark

TRIVIA

Q IN ADDITION TO GREETING CARDS, J.C. HALL HELPED CREATE THIS PRODUCT THAT'S OFTEN USED DURING THE HOLIDAYS AND SPECIAL OCCASIONS.

Answer **WRAPPING PAPER**

GUESTS CAN WATCH AND INTERACT WITH HALLMARK ARTISTS AND WRITERS EACH AFTERNOON INSIDE THE HALLMARK VISITORS CENTER IN KANSAS CITY, MISSOURI.

would create over 150 jobs and make J.C. Hall a very wealthy man. He eventually retired in 1966 and focused on restoring the aging neighborhood that surrounded Hallmark's company headquarters. Hall privately financed and designed one of the most recognizable neighborhoods in the Midwest, Crown Center.

Today, the company has over 27,000 employees and is the most recognized brand in an industry that sells over six billion greeting cards each year.

The Hallmark Visitors Center shares the entire rich history of Hallmark and displays many unique artifacts from their storied past. Exhibits include a collection of one-of-a-kind Christmas trees made for J.C. Hall. You'll see how cards are produced, watch how a machine makes plastic bows, and have the opportunity to meet staff artists. Each afternoon, Hallmark Live features actual sculptors, writers, and designers who create Hallmark products.

HALLMARK VISITORS CENTER
2450 GRAND BLVD., KANSAS CITY, MO 64108
CROWNCENTER.COM

Sam Walton

This boy went from owner of a small shop in the town square in Arkansas to the wealthiest man in America.

Sam Walton was born in 1918 and raised in Missouri. He graduated from the University of Missouri in 1940 with a degree in economics. His first taste of the retail world came while working for J.C. Penney in Des Moines, Iowa. In 1924, he served in the US Army during World War II as an intelligence officer. Upon his return, he gained retail experience by operating multiple Ben Franklin stores.

Walton's 5–10 opened in the town of Bentonville, Arkansas, in 1950. A modest storefront on the downtown square was just what the Walton family wanted after moving to town. But Sam Walton was not destined to settle for just one small store. Nor was he content with chasing after just one dream. Nearly a decade later he'd open the first Walmzart store in the nearby town of Rogers. Walton was 44 years old.

Like most successful dreamers, he was bold, determined, and unafraid of hard work. He also had outside-the-box ideas for cutting costs at his stores. For example, Walton was known to order discontinued floor tiles, even in colors that didn't match, to save a buck. Unlike other retailers, he saw the value in expanding into rural communities.

By all measures, he was brilliant. He even taught himself how to fly with nothing more than a how-to book. He was known to fly around Arkansas scoping out property for new stores and checking up on

Q WHAT FORMER FIRST LADY SERVED SIX YEARS ON WALMART'S BOARD OF DIRECTORS?

Answer HILLARY CLINTON 1986-1992 ★ ★ ★ ★

SAM WALTON'S OFFICE AND DESK, ON DISPLAY AT THE WALMART MUSEUM IN BENTONVILLE, ARKANSAS.

the ones he had already built. One day, Walton spotted a mostly empty Walmart parking lot from the sky and immediately landed his plane to find out why there weren't more customers. It turned out there was a big school festival going on.

Today, Walton's 5–10 is home to The Walmart Museum. You'll see merchandise from the retail giant's early days, along with Sam Walton's office and 1979 Ford pick-up truck. The museum features interactive exhibits and displays detailing Walton's business philosophy. Admission is free. An old-fashioned soda fountain is located next door with ice cream, floats, soda, and other sweet treats. Nearby, the Crystal Bridges Museum of Art is recognized as one of the best art museums in the world. It was funded in large part by Alice Walton, daughter of Sam Walton.

Walmart now has more than 5,000 locations in the United States and employs more than 1.5 million people. The Walton family, through their charitable foundation, donates more than $400 million annually to countless causes including education, the environment, and improving the quality of life in Arkansas.

THE WALMART MUSEUM
105 N MAIN ST., BENTONVILLE, AR 72712
WALMARTMUSEUM.COM

Johnny Morris

A small-town fisherman becomes a billionaire and leading voice for conservation.

Johnny Morris developed a love of bass fishing at the age of 21 while growing up in southwest Missouri. He spent five years as a professional fisherman and started his first Bass Pro Shop in the back of his father's liquor store. He grew his business into 200 retail outlets including the world headquarters in his hometown of Springfield. His products include the Bass Tracker which has been America's most popular fishing boat for over 40 years.

Other Morris-backed projects include Big Cedar Lodge, Bass Pro Shops at the Pyramid in Memphis, and the Wonders of Wildlife attraction.

Wonders of Wildlife was named America's Best Aquarium and Best New Attraction by *USA Today* readers in 2018. The 350,000-square-foot complex is split into two sections: Wildlife Galleries and Aquarium Adventures.

The Wildlife Galleries are incredible replicas of animals and habitats from all across the globe. The 1.5 miles of trails are designed to transport guests through various habitats with changing sights, sounds, temperatures, and even smells. The Great African Hall features scenes of elephants, giraffes, crocodiles, and zebras mingling on the savannah. A mountain mural, covered with 40 wild sheep, towers overhead at Sheep Mountain. You can step into a replica of Theodore Roosevelt's cabin and view some of his personal belongings.

TRIVIA

Q JOHNNY MORRIS GIFTED WHAT US PRESIDENT WITH A FISHING BOAT CALLED *BASS FORCE ONE?*

Answer GEORGE W. BUSH ★ ★ ★ ★ ★ ★

WONDERS OF WILDLIFE IN SPRINGFIELD, MISSOURI, FEATURES BREATHTAKING REPLICAS OF ANIMAL HABITATS FROM ALL OVER THE WORLD.

Conservation is underscored in many of the exhibits including Year of the Bird. Here visitors will learn about the Migratory Bird Treaty Act that protects birds from meaningless killing. One exhibit, the Polar Expedition & Penguin Cove puts you right in the middle of a colony of live penguins.

On the aquarium side, the experience begins in the Great Oceans Hall where you're surrounded by fish to replicate the depths of the ocean. In the Open Ocean exhibit, you'll see over 6,000 herring swimming together in formation. The aquarium features 35,000 live animals including exotic fish, mammals, reptiles, and birds. You'll see over 800 species of sharks, rays, jellies, and eels. A special exhibit highlights some of America's past presidents and their love of fishing.

A welcome video is narrated by Morris and gives visitors a look at his passion for nature and conservation. Guests can also peek into a replica of the store where Morris began his career in 1972. Wonders of Wildlife is home to several additional museums: The National Bass Fishing Hall of Fame, the Bass Pro Shops Motorsports Museum, the National Sporting Arms Museum, and the National Archery Hall of Fame.

WONDERS OF WILDLIFE
500 W SUNSHINE ST., SPRINGFIELD, MO 65807
WONDERSOFWILDLIFE.ORG

Edwin Binney

A man proves listening to your wife's advice might make you a millionaire.

In the late 1800s, Edwin Binney and his cousin C. Harold Smith founded Binney & Smith in New York City. Binney was the inventor and marketer of the duo while Smith was responsible for sales. Their company produced coloring that went into everything from barns to car tires. In 1900, they began producing pencils for students to use on slate boards in classrooms. They also invented dustless chalk, which earned them a gold medal at the 1904 World's Fair. This new chalk was designed so particles would fall to the ground instead of creating a cloud of dust.

Their most transformative invention was a non-toxic crayon. Crayons originated in Europe and had been used mainly for industrial purposes like marking cargo or shipping containers. They were made using a mixture of oil and charcoal and they were mostly black. In time, they added powders to make various colors.

Edwin Binney's wife was a schoolteacher. She suggested that the company look into making an inexpensive alternative for imported crayons that would also be safe for children. After experimenting, company researchers learned that wax could replace oil and make a sturdier, non-toxic crayon. Mrs. Binney was French and named this new product Crayola which translates to "oily stick of chalk."

The first set of crayons included eight different colors. These were sold door-to-door for just a nickel per box. The box was expanded to 48 colors in 1949 and then 64 colors by 1958. That year, the newest

TRIVIA

Q CAN YOU NAME THE ORIGINAL EIGHT COLORS FEATURED IN THE FIRST BOX OF CRAYONS?

Answer RED, ORANGE, YELLOW, GREEN, BLUE, VIOLET, BROWN, AND BLACK.

THE CRAYOLA EXPERIENCE IN ORLANDO, FLORIDA.

box featured a crayon sharpener for the first time. By 1993, Crayola was selling a package of 96 colors which was dubbed the Big Box.

Today, Crayola is owned by the Hallmark company and produces 3 billion crayons per year. A 20-acre solar farm powers their world headquarters where 8,500 crayons are made per minute.

The Crayola Experience is a 65,000-square-foot museum with interactive attractions for families. You can name and wrap your very own Crayola crayon, enjoy a 4-D coloring experience, see a live manufacturing exhibition and enjoy 27 hands-on exhibits. The museum's gift shop has the largest selection of Crayola crayons in the world along with unique souvenirs.

While the main location is near Crayola headquarters in Easton, Pennsylvania, there are other Crayola Store locations with similar activities in Minneapolis, Minnesota, Plano, Texas; Chandler, Arizona; and Orlando, Florida.

CRAYOLAEXPERIENCE.COM

George Washington Carver

Born into slavery, the Peanut Man became one of the most important and respected scientists in American history.

George Washington Carver was born a slave in the town of Diamond, Missouri. A week after his birth, he was kidnapped along with his mother and sister. While the young Carver was quickly found and returned to Missouri, his sister and mother were never recovered. After the Civil War, slavery became illegal in Missouri. Carver's former owners decided to keep and raise George and his brother James. They treated them as their own children and taught them to read and write.

Carver was accepted to Highland College in Kansas but denied admittance once it was discovered he was not white. However, that did not stop him from learning about science and conducting his own experiments. He was the first Black student at Iowa State where he studied agriculture. He soon became recognized as a brilliant botanist.

Carver began teaching at Tuskegee University in Alabama in 1896. His research improved the lives of people in the South who had become dependent on the cotton market which was waning. He introduced other cash crops that could be grown in its place

TRIVIA

Q AS CARVER GREW OLDER AND WEAKER, WHAT FAMOUS INNOVATOR PAID TO HAVE AN ELEVATOR INSTALLED IN CARVER'S DORM AT TUSKEGEE?

Answer HENRY FORD, WHO HAD BECOME A CLOSE FRIEND OF CARVER.

THE GEORGE WASHINGTON CARVER CENTER IN AUSTIN, TEXAS.

like soybeans and sweet potatoes. Carver took his findings directly to farmers using a mobile classroom that became known as a Jesup Wagon, named after Morris Jesup who was a major contributor to the university.

During his lifetime, Carver became known as a leading expert in science and advised world leaders on a range of important matters. His most important contribution to society was discovering the many uses of the peanut.

The list of items that Carver was able to produce using peanuts is long and varied. Food products included peanut brittle, instant coffee, pancake flour, mayonnaise, Worcestershire sauce, cooking oil, and evaporated milk. Household items included laundry soap, shampoo, shaving cream, and lotions. On their website, Tuskegee University notes more than 300 products that are credited to Carver's research, including 118 uses for sweet potatoes. The products include molasses, postage stamp glue, flour, vinegar, synthetic rubber, and even a type of gasoline.

Oddly enough, Carver was not the inventor of peanut butter as many people believe. The history of peanut butter extends all the way back to the Ancient Incas and the Aztecs who ground roasted peanuts into a paste. Modern-day peanut butter can be traced to three separate inventors including Dr. John Harvey Kellogg of Kellogg's Cereal.

Carver used most of his life savings to build a museum devoted to his work. Sadly, the museum caught fire in 1949 and most of its exhibits were destroyed, including many of Carver's paintings and drawings. The rebuilt museum in Tuskegee still highlights his historic career. Visitors will see a display that lists more than 300 alternative products that Carver crafted from peanuts, sweet potatoes, and other plants. You will have the opportunity to sample some of those products and see the original canisters from some of them as well. The second section of the museum focuses on the development of Tuskegee Institute. The museum has several statues of Carver, along with many of his awards and plaques.

On the property, visitors have access to the former home of Booker T. Washington. Washington, an accomplished author and educator, hired Carver to teach at Tuskegee University. Washington lived on-site in a house known as The Oaks which was built by students in 1900 using bricks that they manufactured themselves on campus. It was the first house in Macon County to have electricity and steam heating. Washington lived in the house until his death in 1915. The home was acquired by the National Park Service in 1974 and became part of the Tuskegee Institute National Historic Site.

George Washington Carver was the first Black American to be the subject of a national monument. A 210-acre site in Diamond, Missouri, honors Carver in the place where he lived as a child. What was once a plantation is now a museum, nature trails, and a memorial to Carver with a statue in his honor. The Missouri Botanical Gardens in St. Louis opened a George Washington Carver garden in 2005. The focal point of the garden is a six-foot bronze statue of Carver.

Henry Ford

Despite having just an eighth grade education, he forever changed America with his innovative ideas.

Henry Ford was born on a Michigan farm in 1863. He was in his early teens when he first began to tinker and experiment with his own inventions. He became sought after in his neighborhood for taking watches apart and fixing them. He quit school after eighth grade, uninterested in formal education.

Ford is best remembered as the man who introduced the world's first automobile assembly line in 1910. This radical new idea for mass production expanded America's middle class, especially in northern states like Michigan. Ford also created the Model T automobile which resulted in both fame and fortune.

By 1918, the black Model T made up half of the automobiles in the United States. Ford quipped that, "Any customer can have any color they want so long as it's black." Black paint was said to dry faster, and sticking to a single color helped the new cars move along the assembly line more quickly.

The innovative assembly line helped make automobiles affordable for nearly everyone. The Model T initially took nearly 13 hours to build when it was first introduced in 1908. By the mid 1920s, the time had been cut down to 30 seconds resulting in lower prices for consumers. Ford also introduced the five-day, 40-hour work week.

Sadly, Ford's life story is less than perfect. He developed a large ego with his new fame and wealth. The biggest blemish on his legacy

 TRIVIA

FORD DISCOVERED THAT WASTE FROM HIS SAWMILLS COULD BE USED TO PRODUCE WHAT PRODUCT? HINT: THE PRODUCT'S BRAND WAS NAMED AFTER HIS FRIEND EDWARD KINGSFORD.

Answer | **CHARCOAL**

THE HENRY FORD COLLECTION INCLUDES THE CHAIR ABRAHAM LINCOLN WAS SITTING IN WHEN HE WAS SHOT AT THE FORD THEATER AS WELL AS THE LIMO JOHN F. KENNEDY WAS RIDING IN WHEN HE WAS ASSASSINATED.

was his anti-Jewish rhetoric and propaganda during both World Wars. It wasn't until 1945, after seeing horrifying film clips of a Nazi death camp that Ford was stunned and regretted his actions.

He died at his lavish estate known as Fair Lane in 1947. Today, visitors can tour the property and grounds. It sits on 1,300 acres and was built as Henry and Clara Ford's dream home where he lived for 30 years. It was one of the first sites in America to obtain National Historic Landmark status.

In Dearborn, The Henry Ford (a.k.a. The Henry Ford Museum of American Innovation) is sort of a Disney World for history buffs. It is an incredible collection of rare or one-of-a-kind artifacts relating to American history. One of the signature exhibits is the presidential limousine that John F. Kennedy was riding in when he was assassinated in 1963. The museum also displays the chair Abraham Lincoln was sitting in when he was shot at the Ford Theater in 1865.

Most visitors need several days to fully explore the entire property. The vehicles on display include an 1865 steam-engine Roper, the oldest surviving American car and predecessor to Ford's first gas-powered vehicle. Other stunning beauties include a 1955 Chevrolet Bel Air, the first 1965 Ford Mustang, and a 1931 Bugatti Royale convertible, along with oddities like the original Oscar Mayer Wienermobile. While most vehicles are available simply for viewing, others are more interactive. For example, you can step inside the actual bus that made Rosa Parks a civil rights icon in Montgomery, Alabama.

The Henry Ford features artifacts well beyond its impressive collection of vehicles. Visitors can see tools and machines used in early American agriculture and furniture dating back to 1670. There's an original copy of Thomas Paine's pamphlet *Common Sense* from 1776, a vast display of antique telephones, and even a 1941 Allegheny Steam Locomotive. The locomotive was one of the most powerful ever built and could generate 7,500 horsepower.

Greenfield Village is a living history museum that has been open to the public since 1933. Some of the country's most historic buildings are represented on this 240-acre space located just behind The Henry Ford. One of those buildings is the Wright Brothers' Bicycle Shop where the duo designed the airplane. The shop was moved from its original location in Dayton, Ohio. An exact reproduction of Thomas Edison's Menlo Park lab is one of two significant properties related to the famous inventor. Inside the lab was where Edison worked on inventing the light bulb. You'll also be able to tour Henry Ford's own birthplace and see a replica of the factory where he built his first automobile.

For a unique tour of Greenfield Village, hop into a working vintage Model T and take a ride with one of the museum's tour guides. They'll show you around and give you a first-hand look at how these early vehicles helped change the course of American history.

HENRY FORD'S FAIR LANE ESTATE
1 FAIR LANE DR., DEARBORN, MI 48128
HENRYFORDFAIRLANE.ORG

THE HENRY FORD-MUSEUM, GREENFIELD VILLAGE, & ROUGE FACTORY
20900 OAKWOOD BLVD., DEARBORN, MI 48124
THEHENRYFORD.ORG

The Wright Brothers

From selling bicycles to creating an airplane, their dedication forever changed how we travel.

Wilbur and Orville Wright were brothers and two of seven children born to Milton and Susan Wright. The two boys were inseparable and the best of friends. Both brothers attended high school, though they never received diplomas. Together, they opened a printing press and later a bicycle shop, which expanded to six locations in Dayton, Ohio.

In 1896, the Wright Brothers launched their own line of bicycles. The profits from their stores helped fund their interest in aviation. While others had already worked on gliders, Wilbur and Orville researched and experimented to find out why earlier flights had not been successful. They initially concluded that early airplanes required pilots to shift their bodies to control the plane. Later they learned that the plane could better be controlled by moving its wings.

While their early research and designs took place in Dayton, their experiments and first successful flight happened in Kitty Hawk, North Carolina. The airplane now included a lightweight engine made of aluminum. On December 17, 1903, Orville Wright manned the first flight. On the fourth attempt of the day, their plane flew 852 feet, staying in the air for just under one minute. The brothers founded American Wright Company and became trailblazers in the aviation industry.

Wilbur and Orville designed a house they planned to share in the Oakville neighborhood of Dayton. Wilbur died of typhoid fever at age 45, before construction had even started on the estate known as Hawthorne Hill. Instead, Orville, his sister Katharine, and their father

TRIVIA

Q HOW LONG DID THE WRIGHT BROTHERS' FIRST SUCCESSFUL MACHINE-POWERED FLIGHT LAST AT KITTY HAWK, NORTH CAROLINA?

Answer | 120 FEET IN 12 SECONDS |

ORVILLE WRIGHT'S MANSION IN DAYTON IS PERIODICALLY OPEN TO THE PUBLIC FOR TOURS. INSIDE YOU'LL SEE PERSONAL BELONGINGS INCLUDING HIS FAVORITE CHAIR.

Milton all lived in the house. These days, the Wright Brothers' family home may be best known as a tourist attraction or the place where local kids go sledding after a snowstorm. But in 1914, Hawthorn Hill was welcoming some of America's most famous people: Henry Ford, Thomas Edison, and Charles Lindbergh were among the famous houseguests. Ronald Reagan stayed in the home in later years as have many other celebrities.

If you're lucky enough to catch a tour of the property, you'll notice that many of the items still inside belonged to the Wright family. Even Orville's bed and favorite reading chair are inside. There have only been three owners since it was built.

Orville's room is essentially the same as it was when he lived there, including his books and furniture. Other notable features of the home include a rare wrap-around shower on the second floor. It was technically known as a needle shower and was found mostly in the homes of rich and famous people of the time. The house became known as Hawthorn Hill because of the abundance of Hawthorn trees on the property. The house had five bedrooms, four bathrooms, servant's quarters, and a full basement and attic.

Tours of the home are offered throughout the year on Wednesdays and Saturdays, but prepaid reservations are required. You can book a tour through the Carillon Historical Park website. While you're visiting the park, be sure to check out a restored 1905 Wright Flyer III.

This was considered the first practical flying machine because it was able to take off, fly for a considerable length of time, and land safely. The historical park also displays the patent for the flying machine.

The original Wright Cycle Company building was relocated in 1937 to The Henry Ford Museum in Dearborn, Michigan. However, the Wright's third shop was preserved and can be toured at the Dayton Aviation Heritage National Historical Park. The park is operated by the National Park Service.

Other noteworthy sites in the Dayton area include the Huffman Prairie Flying Field which served as the airport where the Wright Brothers first tested their planes. You can also visit the National Museum of the US Air Force which has a Wright 1909 Military Flyer on display. The museum is the world's largest military airplane museum and includes four hangars of exhibits including a Boeing VC-137C SAM 26000. The aircraft, best known as Air Force One, flew several US presidents from 1962–1998. It served as the official plane for Kennedy and Johnson before becoming a back-up plane for Nixon, Ford, Carter, Reagan, Bush, and Clinton.

Both brothers are buried at the Woodland Cemetery in Dayton. A memorial and National Park Service visitors center also exists in Kitty Hawk, North Carolina, where the Wrights experimented and later achieved their first successful machine-powered flight.

DAYTON AVIATION HERITAGE NATIONAL HISTORICAL PARK
16 S WILLIAMS ST., DAYTON, OH 45402
NPS.GOV/DAAV

WRIGHT BROTHERS NATIONAL MEMORIAL
1000 N CROATAN HWY., KILL DEVIL HILLS, NC 27948
NPS.GOV/WRBR

One of the Wright Brothers original
bicycle shops in Dayton, Ohio (page 84)

"Big Bird" is one of Jim Henson's Muppets on display at the Center for Puppetry Arts in Atlanta, Georgia (page 43)

An early Dr Pepper bottle on exhibit at the Dr Pepper Museum in Waco, Texas (page 156)

ONE GALLON

Dr Pepper®

FOUNTAIN – VENDING SYRUP

MANUFACTURED BY
Dr Pepper Company

The Ca' d'Zan mansion where John
Ringling, of The Ringling Brothers, lived
with his wife in Sarasota, Florida (page 49)

An Andy Griffith statue in his hometown of Mount Airy, North Carolina (page 12)

Muhammad Ali's boxing robe on display at the Ali Center in Louisville, Kentucky (page 144)

The Walmart Museum, located in
Sam Walton's original 5&10 store in
Bentonville, Arkansas (page 72)

Billy Graham's traveling pulpit, equipped with warning lights to give him time cues (page 120)

Dolly Parton's "coat of many colors" on display at Dollywood in Pigeon Forge, Tennessee (page 4)

A recreation of the shed where Harley-Davidson
began operations in Milwaukee, Wisconsin (page 64)

A statue of Elvis Presley in Memphis, Tennessee (page 16)

Antique
Please
Be Gentle

JOHN DEERE

Vintage John Deere equipment on display at the
John Deere Pavilion in Moline, Illinois (page 62)

George Eastman lived in this mansion from 1905-1932. Today it houses the world's oldest museum dedicated to photography and is open to the public for tours. *Courtesy: Library of Congress*

George Eastman

A self-educated dreamer made saving memories possible for all of us.

George Eastman spent most of his life in Rochester, New York. He was largely self-educated with a great mind for business and innovation. He became interested in amateur photography in his early 20s but wasn't fond of having to haul heavy equipment or the high cost of it. Eastman was also less than thrilled with the expense of having to develop the photos.

For three years, Eastman experimented in his mother's kitchen and made a discovery that would forever change the industry. In 1880, at the age of 26, he had perfected the process of making dry plates for photography. The dry plate would allow the photographer to store it until it was ready to be used for a picture and then store it again before developing it in a dark room.

Kodak, a brand name completely made up by Eastman, would begin to offer box cameras to the public in 1888. This invention gave the average person an opportunity to take pictures. Each camera came with 100 exposures and could be sent back to company headquarters in Rochester to be developed and reloaded with new film. Their slogan was "You press the button. We do the rest."

Eastman introduced roll film in 1889 which has remained the standard ever since. Thomas Edison used Eastman's film in his motion pictures from 1847–1931. "Kodak moment" became a familiar phrase for anyone taking a picture they deemed worth saving.

TRIVIA

Q WHAT SINGER HAD A TOP-10 HIT WITH THE SONG "KODACHROME"?

Answer **PAUL SIMON** ★ ★ ★ ★ ★ ★ ★

During his career, Eastman cared about his employees. He was the first in the nation to offer workers shares in company profits and a believer in promoting women as well.

In the late 1920s, Eastman was diagnosed with an irreversible spinal disease, and on March 14, 1932, he ended his own life. He left behind a note for his friends that said, "My work is done. Why wait?" He also left behind a world he helped change for the better with his innovations and charity. Eastman donated more than $100 million to educational and arts institutions, public parks, hospitals, dental clinics, and charitable organizations around the world.

In addition to its discoveries and innovations in the world of photography, Eastman had also provided assistance to the US government during World War I. His laboratory helped build up America's chemical industry so that it no longer needed to rely on Germany.

The Eastman Kodak Company remained the dominant photography business during most of the 20th century. As late as 1976, Kodak enjoyed 90 percent of film sales and 85 percent of camera sales. Despite being the first company to introduce a self-contained digital camera, the trend to all-digital technology took a toll on Kodak. It filed for bankruptcy in 2012.

Constructed at the beginning of the 20th century, Eastman's primary residence has become the George Eastman Museum which gives visitors a personal look at one of America's most notable innovators. Eastman's lavish mansion has been restored and preserved along with its gardens. Most of the home is open to public viewing. You can explore the dining, living, and billiard rooms, along with the Eastman's library. As you walk up the grand staircase to view the second floor, catch a glimpse of the Aeolian pipe organ which has more than 6,000 pipes and is connected throughout the house with hundreds of miles of wiring. The third floor once housed Eastman's screening room and workshop, as well as living quarters for household staff. Museum members can go behind the scenes to the third floor and to the basement. The mansion's multiple gardens are

THE LIVING ROOM IN GEORGE EASTMAN'S MANSION IN ROCHESTER. NEW YORK.

regularly used for functions in Rochester and shouldn't be missed if you tour the property.

The George Eastman Museum preserves and promotes the art of film in all its forms. The collection contains more than 28,000 titles spanning the entire history of international cinema. The museum stores original Technicolor negatives of American film classics like *The Wizard of Oz* and *Gone with the Wind*. Its archives contain over four million film stills, posters, and historical documents.

For photography lovers, the museum displays rare cameras, equipment, and early photographs. You'll also see some of the initial Kodak promotional materials and products.

Eastman was laid to rest at a memorial in the Eastman Business Park in Rochester.

EASTMAN MUSEUM
900 E AVE., ROCHESTER. NY 14607
EASTMAN.ORG

MADE IN THE USA

HISTORICAL FIGURES
& CULTURAL ICONS

★ FINDING THE AMERICAN DREAM ★

Neil Armstrong

His dreams traveled from beyond Ohio to the surface of the moon.

Neil Armstrong was born in Wapakoneta, Ohio, in 1935. His love of flying started early in life after his father took him to see the National Air Races in Cleveland. Neil's first experience in a plane came around age five when he rode in a Ford Trimotor, also known as the Tin Goose. He began taking flying lessons in 1944, earning a student flight certificate on his 16th birthday. Armstrong could legally fly before he was able to drive.

He attended college at Purdue University as part of the Holloway Plan. The government program provided applicants with two years of study, followed by two years of flight training and one year of service in the US Navy as an aviator. Once completed, applicants would then finish the final two years of their bachelor's degree.

Armstrong served in the US Navy, becoming the youngest person to serve in the V-F 51, all-jet squadron. During his time in the service, he flew 78 missions during the Korean War, totaling 121 hours in the air. One mission resulted in Armstrong ejecting himself from his plane after flying through a booby trap that damaged the wing. His last mission was on March 5, 1952. His military service resulted in distinguished honors including the Air Medal, two gold stars, the Korean Service Medal, the National Service Defense Medal, and the United Nations Korea Medal.

After college, Armstrong worked as an experimental research test pilot. During his career, he flew over 200 different types of aircraft.

TRIVIA

 **IN 2005, NEIL ARMSTRONG THREATENED TO SUE MIKE SIZEMORE OF LEBANON, OHIO, AFTER HE WAS CAUGHT TRYING TO SELL WHAT?**

Answer **ARMSTRONG'S HAIR!**

THE CUSTOM AIRSTREAM TRAILER WHERE THE APOLLO 11 CREW WAS QUARANTINED UPON RETURNING FROM THE MOON IS ON DISPLAY AT THE NATIONAL AIR AND SPACE MUSEUM.

In 1962, Armstrong applied to be part of Project Gemini and became the first civilian astronaut. The biggest achievement in his career began on July 16, 1969. Apollo 11 launched from the Kennedy Space Center and five days later, Armstrong became the first person to walk on the surface of the moon. His words as he stepped off the ladder and onto the moon would forever be part of American history: "That's one small step for [a] man, one giant leap for mankind."

After the mission, the crew of Apollo 11 was quarantined for 18 days. Part of that time was spent in a specially modified Airstream trailer. That trailer is on display at the Smithsonian's Air and Space Museum. An estimated six million people celebrated the achievement of Armstrong, Buzz Aldrin, and Michael Collins at ticker tape parades in New York and Chicago. President Richard Nixon awarded all three of them the Presidential Medal of Freedom.

The Armstrong Air & Space Museum is located in Armstrong's hometown of Wapakoneta, Ohio. The uniquely shaped building displays artifacts relating to Armstrong's life and career as well as exhibits about the history of space travel. The museum is a concrete building that at first glance appears to be underground. Armstrong was on hand for the ribbon cutting ceremony when it opened in 1972, exactly three years after his historic walk on the moon.

Among the exhibits on display are three aircraft piloted by Armstrong including an F5D Skylancer, an experimental airplane he flew as a Naval test pilot. Other artifacts include the Gemini VIII space capsule, equipment from the Apollo 11 mission, spacesuits, a moon rock, recordings of Armstrong's parents during the Apollo 11 mission, and examples of space food and tools astronauts use to go to the bathroom.

The story of Armstrong's life prior to his career as an astronaut is also shared through personal belongings like his grade school lunchbox and a childhood science project. Visitors will also learn about the race to the moon in chronological order beginning with a replica of the Soviet Union's Sputnik satellite. Next, you can experience what it's like to roam through space using hands-on simulators. One interactive exhibit allows you to practice landing a space shuttle or docking the Gemini capsule as Armstrong did.

The 56-foot dome in the center of the museum houses the Astro Theater, a unique venue that allows guests to enjoy the 25-minute documentary about Apollo 11's lunar landing.

Armstrong's Apollo 11 mission was launched from the Kennedy Space Center which is located along Florida's Space Coast and is now open for tours. All of the NASA affiliated museums have impressive collections of artifacts and exhibits related to exploring space and visiting the moon. The US Space & Rocket Center is located in Huntsville, Alabama, and the Johnson Space Center is in Houston, Texas.

ARMSTRONG AIR & SPACE
MUSEUM
500 APOLLO DR.,
WAPAKONETA, OH 45895
ARMSTRONGMUSEUM.ORG

US SPACE & ROCKET CENTER
1 TRANQUILITY BASE,
HUNTSVILLE, AL 35805
ROCKETCENTER.COM

THE ARMSTRONG AIR & SPACE MUSEUM IS LOCATED IN NEIL ARMSTRONG'S HOMETOWN OF WAPAKONETA, OHIO.

Rosa Parks

She stood up for something by sitting down.

Rosa Parks was born in Tuskegee, Alabama, in 1913. She grew up on her grandparents' farm in Pine Level, Alabama, following the divorce of her parents. They were both former slaves and strong advocates for racial equality. As a child, Parks witnessed intimidation tactics by the KKK. In later years, Parks recalled seeing her grandfather holding a shotgun in the front yard as Klan members marched down their street.

On December 1, 1955, Parks boarded a city bus after finishing work at a local department store. Soon after, the seats had started to fill, and several white passengers were left standing. The bus driver asked four Black passengers to give up their seats so the whites could be seated. Rosa Parks declined to give up her seat. The police were called, and she was charged with violating Chapter 6, Section 11, of the Montgomery City code. She was released on bail.

The trial sparked what is now known as the Montgomery Bus Boycott. For 381 days, approximately 40,000 Black residents boycotted the city buses. The boycott ended in victory with the US Supreme Court ruling that segregated buses were unconstitutional. While the boycott caused backlash including shootings and bombings, it helped pave the way for the civil rights movement.

The Rosa Parks Museum is located in downtown Montgomery on the campus of Troy University. The museum is dedicated to telling

TRIVIA

Q ROSA PARKS WAS NOT THE FIRST PERSON TO BE ARRESTED FOR NOT GIVING UP A BUS SEAT. WHAT WAS THE NAME OF THE 15-YEAR-OLD GIRL WHO DID THE SAME THING NINE MONTHS BEFORE PARKS?

Answer **CLAUDETTE COLVIN**

LEFT: THE ACTUAL BUS SHE WAS RIDING IS ON DISPLAY AT THE HENRY FORD MUSEUM IN DEARBORN, MICHIGAN. *RIGHT*: A HISTORICAL MARKER IN MONTGOMERY, ALABAMA, MARKS THE SPOT WHERE ROSA PARKS WAS ARRESTED.

the story of Parks as well as others behind the bus boycott. Visitors will hear first-hand stories from those on the front lines of the civil rights movement in the 1950s. Exhibits include Parks's original fingerprint arrest record, court documents, and a restored 1955 station wagon known as a rolling church. The rolling churches were used to transport protestors.

Historical markers are located on the streets that indicate the route of the bus and the spot where the arrest took place.

The actual bus, #2857, is on display at the Henry Ford Museum in Dearborn, Michigan. The bus had been purchased in the early 1970s by a Montgomery resident who used it for storing tools in a field. His family, realizing its historical importance, later sold the bus at auction. The winning bid was $492,000. The museum then began the costly process of restoring the bus to its original condition. It was unveiled to the public in 2003 in the museum's With Liberty and Justice for All exhibit.

Rosa Parks died in 2005 at the age of 92. She was laid to rest at Woodlawn Cemetery in Detroit.

Harriet Tubman

Born into slavery, she made the dream of freedom possible for herself and many others.

Harriet Tubman was born into slavery in Dorchester County, Maryland. Her dream of freedom came in 1849 after escaping to Philadelphia. Her story is inspiring not only because she successfully freed herself but also because she put her own safety and freedom on the line to help save others as a "conductor" on the Underground Railroad—a series of churches, schoolhouses, and private homes where slaves could hide en route to safe states or to Canada.

Though some of the most familiar photos of Tubman show her as an elderly woman, she was actually quite young during the time she helped to rescue escaping slaves. Her exact age has always been a mystery considering that while her birth certificate lists 1815 as the year of her birth, her grave site says 1820, and Tubman herself claimed to have been born in 1825.

Tubman was incredibly sophisticated and took many minor details into account during her time as an Underground Railroad conductor. After making contact with escaping slaves, she made sure that they did not leave town until Saturday evening because the newspapers wouldn't print runaway notices before Monday morning. Tubman herself used various tricks and disguises to go unnoticed. Sometimes she walked around with chickens pretending to work or read a newspaper (despite being illiterate). Over the course of a decade, her efforts helped free more than 70 slaves. Her last mission was in 1860.

TRIVIA

Q LEADING UP TO THE CIVIL WAR, TUBMAN NEVER FAILED TO COMPLETE A SINGLE RESCUE MISSION, EARNING HER WHAT SPECIAL NICKNAME?

Answer **MOSES**

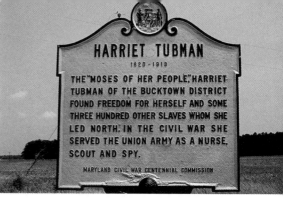

Tubman was notoriously tough and she always carried a pistol. During the Civil War, she worked as a nurse and spy for the Union Army. During surgery for a brain injury later in life, she refused anesthesia and instead bit down on a bullet.

THE 125-MILE HARRIET TUBMAN BYWAY ALLOWS VISITORS TO GAIN INSIGHT INTO THE CIVIL RIGHTS TRAILBLAZER.

She became frail by 1911 and moved into the very nursing home that she helped found years earlier. The Tubman Home for Aged and Indigent Negroes ran until the early 1920s. It has since been restored as a museum in Tubman's honor and is now open for tours in Auburn, New York.

Travelers can also explore the 125-mile Tubman Byway that takes visitors on a journey along Maryland's eastern shore to highlight the historic moments of her life and accomplishments. The drive extends on through Delaware and ends in Philadelphia where Tubman initially gained her freedom. There are 36 historical sites along the byway. One highlight is the Harriet Tubman Underground Railroad Visitors Center which opened in 2017. There is also a separate Harriet Tubman Museum located in Cambridge, Maryland.

HARRIET TUBMAN HOUSE
180 SOUTH ST., AUBURN, NY 13021
HARRIETTUBMANHOME.COM

HARRIET TUBMAN UNDERGROUND
RAILROAD NATIONAL MONUMENT
4068 GOLDEN HILL RD., CHURCH
CREEK, MD 21622
NPS.GOV/HATU

HARRIET TUBMAN MUSEUM
424 RACE ST., CAMBRIDGE, MD 21613
HARRIETTUBMANBYWAY.ORG

Martin Luther King, Jr.

A gifted leader brought civil rights to the attention of an entire nation.

Martin Luther King, Jr. was a preacher, public speaker, and organizer who became the leader of America's civil rights movement. Born and raised in Georgia, his family was deeply religious. However, King didn't always adhere to his family's religious ideals. Only after taking a Bible class during his junior year of high school did he agree to follow his father's footsteps into ministry with a renewed faith in God. His father was the pastor of Atlanta's Ebenezer Baptist Church where King became a co-pastor at the age of 19.

King graduated from Morehouse College in 1948 and then attended Crozer Theological Seminary in Chester, Pennsylvania, where he was class valedictorian in 1951. King met Coretta Scott while working on his doctorate at Boston University. They were married in 1953.

King's first job after college was preaching at Dexter Avenue Baptist Church in Montgomery, Alabama. During his time as pastor, a local woman named Rosa Parks made headlines after being arrested. She had refused to give up her seat on a bus to a white person. Dr. King worked with local civil rights leaders to organize a Montgomery bus boycott. The boycott propelled King as a leader in the movement and brought fresh new attention to race relations in America.

TRIVIA

Q **BESIDES KING, WHO IS THE ONLY OTHER AMERICAN TO HAVE HAD HIS BIRTHDAY CELEBRATED AS A NATIONAL HOLIDAY?**

Answer **GEORGE WASHINGTON**

DR. MARTIN LUTHER KING

(Continued from other side)

Dr. King became pastor of Dexter Avenue Baptist Church in September, 1954. He led the Bus Boycott of 1955-56 as president of the Montgomery Improvement Association. Leaving Montgomery in 1960 he went on to national leadership in civil rights, advocating non-violence. Accomplishments include: president of the Southern Christian Leadership Conference; Selma-Montgomery March; March on Washington; Nobel Peace Prize. His work brought on a world social-humanitarian movement. He was assassinated on April 4, 1968 in Memphis, Tennessee, during an effort to secure laborers' rights.

THE HOME WHERE MARTIN LUTHER KING, JR. LIVED WHILE SERVING AS A PASTOR IN MONTGOMERY, ALABAMA.

During his life, King would be arrested multiple times and constantly subjected to attacks. He organized gatherings and protests that would gain national attention. In 1963, he led a march in Washington, D.C., that drew over 200,000 people. At the Lincoln Memorial, King delivered what's now known as the "I Have A Dream" speech. In that speech, King said: "I have a dream that my four children will one day live in a nation where they will not be judged by the color of their skin but by the content of their character."

King helped pass the Civil Rights Act of 1964 and later won a Nobel Peace Prize for his work. The next few years were discouraging for King who had grown tired of the constant criticism and threats against him and his family. In 1968, King delivered a speech in Memphis that promised his supporters that "we will get to the promised land." The next day, he was shot and killed.

The Lorraine Motel was the site of Martin Luther King, Jr.'s assassination. King was standing on the balcony outside of room 306 when he was shot by James Earl Ray. The motel was transformed into the National Civil Rights Museum in 1991. In 2012, it reopened after going through $27.5 million worth of renovations and additions. The facility is sanctioned as a Smithsonian affiliate and offers an impressive depth of history relating to the American civil rights movement.

Near the end of your tour, you'll walk past the room King had been staying in and where he eventually died. You'll also stand just steps from the balcony railing where the assassination took place. Looking down from the balcony as other tourists glance back up in your direction is a powerful moment. A flowered, white and red wreath marks the spot of the shooting.

The museum has art displays, more than 40 films, and various listening stations. There's a replica of the bus Rosa Parks rode, and a reproduction of a Greyhound bus that was set on fire by white supremacists during the Freedom Rides. Vintage vehicles parked outside the building are relevant to the time period but have no significant tie to the hotel or to Dr. King.

King is laid to rest in Atlanta, Georgia, at the Martin Luther King, Jr. National Historical Park. A reflection pool and an eternal flame have been placed across from his grave. His childhood home is a short walk down the street, and available to tour on a first-come, first-served basis. Tickets are distributed fairly quickly, so it's best to arrive early. The ranger-led tour gives you a look inside the home where King lived until he was 12 years old.

A highlight of the park is Ebenezer Baptist Church where King gave his first sermon and became co-pastor with his father in 1960. This was also the site of his funeral in 1968. Inside the sanctuary, you'll hear the words of Dr. King over loudspeakers as you take a seat in one of the original church pews. The stained glass windows and the lighted sign out front have been fully restored.

MARTIN LUTHER KING, JR. NATIONAL HISTORIC PARK
450 AUBURN AVE. NE. ATLANTA. GA 30312
NPS.GOV/MALU

NATIONAL CIVIL RIGHTS MUSEUM
450 MULBERRY ST.. MEMPHIS. TN 38103
CIVILRIGHTSMUSEUM.ORG

MARTIN LUTHER KING. JR.'S MONTGOMERY HOME
DEXTER PARSONAGE MUSEUM
309 S JACKSON ST.. MONTGOMERY. AL 36104
DEXTERKINGMEMORIAL.ORG

MARTIN LUTHER KING, JR
JAN 15, 1929   APR 4, 1968
FOUNDING PRESIDENT
SOUTHERN CHRISTIAN LEADERSHIP CONFERENCE
THEY SAID ONE TO ANOTHER...
BEHOLD, HERE COMETH THE DREAMER...
LET US SLAY HIM...
AND WE SHALL SEE WHAT WILL BECOME OF HIS DREAM
GENESIS 37-19
RALPH DAVID ABERNATHY

EBENEZER
BAPTIST
CHURCH

EBENEZER BAPTIST CHURCH IN ATLANTA AND
THE LORRAINE MOTEL IN MEMPHIS, NOW PART OF
THE NATIONAL CIVIL RIGHTS MUSEUM.

Billy Graham

A decent man who inspired billions of people with his message of hope and faith.

Billy Graham was one of the most respected and influential evangelical leaders in American history. He was a spiritual advisor to every US president from Harry Truman to Barack Obama. Graham was named Gallup's Most Admired Man a record 61 times. At the peak of his popularity, he preached to stadiums that were full to capacity and delivered sermons of hope and inspiration to millions through radio and television.

The Billy Graham Library in Charlotte, North Carolina, is the area's top attraction. Graham was arguably the most famous resident of the state and his life story is masterfully told through engaging exhibits in the library's museum.

You can take a tour of his childhood home (which was moved to the property in 2007) and see the family's kitchen where Graham first told his mother about his newfound faith in God as a teenager.

Inside the museum, visitors walk through a winding series of rooms, each telling a different part of Graham's incredible life as a Christian preacher. A talking cow begins your tour, sharing some memories of Graham—known as Billy Frank—as a young kid who used to milk cows on the farm.

Graham's celebrity status and the influence he had are striking. Displays show pictures of him with everyone from Johnny Cash to leaders from around the world to indicate the magnitude of his reach.

TRIVIA

Q WHAT US PRESIDENT HAD TO BORROW $5 FROM BILLY GRAHAM FOR A CHURCH OFFERING AND LATER SENT HIM A REIMBURSEMENT CHECK?

Answer RICHARD NIXON—AND THE CHECK IS ON DISPLAY IN THE MUSEUM!

GRAHAM'S CHILDHOOD HOME IS LOCATED AT THE BILLY GRAHAM LIBRARY IN CHARLOTTE. INSIDE THE MUSEUM YOU'LL SEE PERSONAL BELONGINGS INCLUDING HIS MODEST OFFICE DESK AND CHAIR.

He preached to hundreds of millions of people during his lifetime. A large poster shows his biggest single gathering in South Korea where more than three million people attended a sermon.

One noteworthy sight that isn't actually in the museum is Graham's office furniture. Tucked away in the corner of a gift shop is the desk and chair that the preacher used during his lifetime. The chair was not fancy and looks to be falling apart. It's quite a contrast from the wealthy appearance that many high-profile evangelical leaders have today. By all accounts, Graham lived a very modest life. The museum staff members who knew him personally are all too happy to point out that he was a decent, down-to-earth person.

Graham and his wife Ruth are buried on-site in a serene garden with a walking path in the shape of a cross. Admission to the Billy Graham Library is always free. While at the museum, you can also pick up a map of other Graham-related sites around the Charlotte area.

BILLY GRAHAM LIBRARY
4330 WESTMONT DR., CHARLOTTE, NC. 28217
BILLYGRAHAMLIBRARY.ORG

Babe Ruth

He was a troubled youth who grew up to become the greatest baseball player of all time.

George Herman Ruth was born and raised in Baltimore and by all accounts had a troubled childhood and youth. As an adult, Ruth openly admitted that he often skipped school, roamed the streets, and would chew tobacco and drink beer when his father wasn't looking. In 1902, Ruth was sent to St. Mary's Industrial School for Boys after his parents ran out of ideas of how to discipline their son.

Ruth was introduced to baseball as a teenager and became a professional player at age 19 with the minor league Baltimore Orioles. Team owner, Jack Dunn became Ruth's legal guardian. That led to jokes that Ruth was "Dunn's new babe." He quickly became known as Babe Ruth.

Ruth later played for the Boston Red Sox and was then traded to the New York Yankees. That trade would be called the Curse of the Bambino as the Red Sox did not win another World Series for 86 years. The Yankees meanwhile went on to win seven pennants and four World Series after having won zero championships prior to Ruth joining the team.

Before retiring in 1935, Ruth had hit 714 career home runs.

The Babe Ruth Birthplace and Museum is located in Baltimore, just a short walk from Oriole Park at Camden Yards. The museum is situated in the row house where George Herman Ruth was born on

TRIVIA

Q BABE RUTH WAS ONE OF THE FIRST FIVE PLAYERS TO BE INDUCTED INTO THE BASEBALL HALL OF FAME. CAN YOU NAME THE OTHER FOUR PLAYERS WHO JOINED HIM IN 1936?

Answer TY COBB. WALTER JOHNSON. CHRISTY MATHEWSON. HONUS WAGNER

THE BABE RUTH BIRTHPLACE AND MUSEUM IS LOCATED IN BALTIMORE. MARYLAND. IT'S A SHORT WALK FROM ORIOLE PARK AT CAMDEN YARDS.

February 6, 1895. The upstairs bedroom where his mother Katherine gave birth to him is part of the tour.

The museum first opened in 1973 with help from Ruth's widow, Claire, and his two daughters who helped select items for the collection. The museum underwent an extensive makeover in 2015 and now features Babe's 1914 rookie baseball card and his Catholic rosary. Visitors can experience the Called Shot Home Run Theater and a display on Ruth's favorite radio program: *The Lone Ranger.* The exhibit includes the radio Ruth listened to in his New York Riverside Drive apartment as well as the complete Lone Ranger costume worn by actor Clayton Moore for the 1950s television series.

The National Baseball Hall of Fame in Cooperstown displays one of the most famous jerseys Ruth ever wore. The jersey was shown in the iconic Nat Fein photo of Babe Ruth standing on the field at Yankee Stadium in 1948 when his No. 3 was officially retired. Ruth was inducted into the very first Hall of Fame class in 1936.

BABE RUTH BIRTHPLACE MUSEUM
216 EMORY ST.. BALTIMORE. MD 21230
BABERUTHMUSEUM.ORG

Meriwether Lewis & William Clark

Together, they survived an 8,000-mile journey exploring the American frontier.

In 1803, Thomas Jefferson selected his personal secretary, Meriwether Lewis, to lead an expedition out West and research the newly purchased Louisiana Territory. Lewis enlisted the help of William Clark who would become his co-leader. The two shared duties equally along the rigorous journey to the Pacific Ocean and back. Their travels lasted from August 31, 1803 to September 25, 1806. Upon their return, they produced journals, maps, and sketches of the discoveries they had made along the way.

Of all the individuals profiled in this book, no one has more historic sites and museums dedicated to him/her than Lewis and Clark. There are dozens of sites in at least 20 states that share a portion of their incredible story. One of the notable stops is the Lewis & Clark Historical Site in Hartford, Illinois. This was where Camp Dubois was settled and their journey began east of the Mississippi River. It was a working military base that has been recreated just south of the original site that is no longer accessible. It was to this camp that Clark recruited men who were known as good hunters and who had well-honed survival skills and trained them for the rigorous journey ahead.

TRIVIA

Q WHAT WAS THE MAIN REASON JEFFERSON ORDERED LEWIS AND CLARK'S EXPEDITION?

Answer TO FIND OUT IF A WATER ROUTE ACROSS THE CONTINENT TO THE PACIFIC OCEAN EXISTS. IT DOESN'T.

A state-of-the-art museum dedicated to westward expansion sits below the Gateway Arch National Monument in St. Louis. After undergoing a massive remodeling and multi-million-dollar upgrade, it gives a compelling look into the Louisiana Purchase and exploration of the West with videos and interactive exhibits.

Another cool stop is Pompeys Pillar National Monument in Billings, Montana. It preserves the only remaining physical evidence of the Lewis and Clark Expedition. On the face of the 150-foot butte, Clark carved his name and the date during his return to what was then the United States. The rock and signature appear on the trail today as they did back in 1806. "Pompey" was the nickname Clark had given to Sacagawea's son.

The Columbia Gorge Discovery Center in The Dalles, Oregon, has done fascinating research on the cargo that Lewis and Clark brought for their journey. The center has a one-of-a-kind exhibit produced by researcher Ken Karsmizki who spent 16 years studying the expedition. His findings led to a Discovery Channel documentary called *The Search for Lewis and Clark* which debuted in 2002.

Meriwether Lewis died in 1809. His burial site is marked with a memorial along the Natchez Trace Parkway at milepost 385.9. William Clark died in 1838 and was laid to rest at Bellefontaine Cemetery in St. Louis.

LEWIS AND CLARK HISTORICAL
SITE: CAMP DUBOIS
1 LEWIS AND CLARK TRAIL.
HARTFORD. IL 62048
CAMPDUBOIS.COM

POMPEYS PILLAR
3039 US HWY. 312.
POMPEYS PILLAR. MT 59064
POMPEYSPILLAR.ORG

COLUMBIA GORGE DISCOVERY CENTER AND MUSEUM
5000 DISCOVERY DR.. THE DALLES. OR 97058
GORGEDISCOVERY.ORG

Buffalo Bill

He gave many Americans their first look at the wild, wild West.

William Cody was born in LeClaire, Iowa, in 1846. As a young boy, he learned to herd cattle and drive a wagon train when his family moved to Kansas. He joined the Pony Express in 1860 and became a scout for the Army following the Civil War. He earned the nickname "Buffalo Bill" as a hunter.

His show business career started in 1872 after starring in a drama called *Scouts of the Prairie*. Cody formed his own troupe—the Buffalo Bill Combination—and performed a variety of plays until 1882. The plays helped to change public opinion about cowboys who were often thought of as dirty, coarse, cattle drivers. The performances in Buffalo Bill's Wild West shows proved that cowboys had admirable skills like roping and bronco riding.

Buffalo Bill had an evolving relationship with Native Americans during the course of his life. In later years, he was an outspoken advocate for American Indians and was known to treat them with respect and as equals when they performed in his Wild West shows. Bill forged an unlikely friendship with Indian Chief Sitting Bull who had been part of his show.

The Wild West Show traveled around the country and then the world to showcase shooting competitions, animals, and reenactments of historical events. The shows were popular and ran until 1913, shortly after Cody was tricked into signing a contract that demoted himself. When he died in 1917, an estimated 20,000 people attended

TRIVIA

 Q WHAT FAMOUS FEMALE SHARPSHOOTER WAS PART OF BUFFALO BILL'S SHOW IN 1889 WHEN SHE EARNED MORE MONEY THAN ANY OF THE OTHER PERFORMERS?

Answer **ANNIE OAKLEY**

BUFFALO BILL'S HOME IN NORTH PLATTE, NEBRASKA, IS OPEN FOR TOURS. HIS LEGACY IS ALSO PRESERVED IN SEVERAL MUSEUMS AROUND THE UNITED STATES.

his funeral. At his request, Buffalo Bill was buried on Lookout Mountain above Denver with a view of the Rocky Mountains.

The Buffalo Bill Museum in Golden, Colorado, shares exhibits about his life and career with rare artifacts like the Stetson hat worn during Bill's last performance. Other items to see include the peace pipe that belonged to Sitting Bull and promotional posters and photographs related to the Wild West Show. Another exhibit highlights the use of firearms.

The history of Buffalo Bill is also preserved at other museums including The Buffalo Bill Museum in LeClaire, Iowa, and the Buffalo Bill Center of the West in Cody, Wyoming.

The Buffalo Bill Ranch State Historical Park in North Platte, Nebraska, is the site of Cody's home from 1886–1913. The property includes the house, a large barn, and public camping sites. His home in Cody, Wyoming, is now a bed and breakfast.

BUFFALO BILL MUSEUM
199 N FRONT ST.,
LECLAIRE, IA 52753
BUFFALOBILLMUSEUMLECLAIRE.COM

THE BUFFALO BILL MUSEUM & GRAVE
987 LOOKOUT MOUNTAIN RD.,
GOLDEN, CO 80401
BUFFALOBILL.ORG

BUFFALO BILL CENTER OF THE WEST
720 SHERIDAN AVE., CODY, WY 82414
CENTEROFTHEWEST.ORG

Abraham Lincoln

He was born poor in a log cabin but is remembered by many as the greatest president in American history.

Abraham Lincoln was born in a small log cabin in Hodgenville, Kentucky, in 1809. As a young man, Lincoln had a thirst for knowledge. His father was said to call him "lazy" because he'd rather read books than work. During his life he became a lawyer, judge, legislator, congressman, and eventually the 16th president of the United States. Lincoln's enduring popularity keeps travelers visiting dozens of historic sites related to his life and career.

The largest concentration of Lincoln-related sites is in Springfield, Illinois, where he lived from 1837–1861. The home where Abraham and Mary Lincoln lived and raised their children for 17 years is a beloved tourist attraction. Guests can walk through the house, observe artifacts that belonged to the Lincoln family, and explore the neighborhood. Nearby sites include Lincoln's tomb at the Oak Ridge Cemetery, the Old State Capitol where he was a legislator, the family church, the Governor's mansion, and the Lincoln-Herndon Law Office. It takes at least half a day to explore the Lincoln Presidential Library and Museum. The galleries house his personal artifacts, special exhibits, and a 4-D movie theater.

Lincoln's biggest memorials, at least in terms of size, are two of the most-visited tourist spots in America. There's Mount Rushmore, where a 60-foot carving of Lincoln's head (among others) attracts nearly three million visitors from around the world each year, and the Lincoln Memorial, dedicated in 1922, which is another larger-

TRIVIA

Q WHERE DID LINCOLN SUPPOSEDLY KEEP HIS IMPORTANT DOCUMENTS?

Answer **INSIDE OF HIS HAT** ★ ★ ★ ★ ★ ★

ONE OF THE BEST PLACES TO SEE HISTORICAL LINCOLN SITES IS IN SPRINGFIELD, ILLINOIS. AROUND TOWN YOU CAN TOUR HIS FAMILY HOME, LAW OFFICE, THE OLD STATE CAPITOL WHERE HE WAS A LEGISLATOR, AND HIS BURIAL TOMB.

than-life monument with a 19-foot-high statue of the 16th president. The memorial sits at the western end of the National Mall, two miles from the US Capitol.

While you're in Washington, D.C., several sites tied to Lincoln are available to tour. The White House is an obvious choice, though tours need to be booked in advance. The cottage where Lincoln spent his summers, located three miles from the White House, is also open for tours.

Visitors can also tour Ford's Theater, where Lincoln was shot on April 14, 1865. The chair where the president was sitting when he was killed is on display at the Henry Ford Museum in Dearborn, Michigan.

Across the street from Ford's Theater is the Petersen House. This is where Lincoln was taken after he had been shot and placed in a bed to be more comfortable. He eventually died there the following morning. Lincoln spent his younger years in both Kentucky and Indiana. The sites where he was born and lived have been designated as memorials.

YOU CAN FIND LINKS TO EVERY ABRAHAM LINCOLN HISTORIC SITE ONLINE AT:
ABRAHAMLINCOLNONLINE.ORG

Georgia O'Keeffe

One of America's most important and successful artists came from humble Wisconsin beginnings.

Georgia O'Keeffe was born in 1887 and grew up on a farm in Wisconsin. She studied at the Art Institute of Chicago and the Arts Students League in New York. Art dealer Alfred Stieglitz gave O'Keeffe her first gallery show in 1916. The two became close and later married in 1924.

In 1929, O'Keeffe made her first visit to northern New Mexico. She came to love the local Navajo culture along with the region's landscape and architecture. She referred to the area as "the faraway" and would visit during the summers to paint. Some of her most notable paintings included: Black Cross, New Mexico; Cow's Skull: Red, White, and Blue; and Ram's Head, White Hollyhock—Hills.

O'Keeffe's artwork is displayed in over 100 public collections in Asia, Europe, and North and Central America. She was known for her paintings of flowers, skyscrapers, animal skulls, and southwestern landscapes. She was also recognized for her work in a male-dominated industry and paved the way for future female artists. O'Keeffe died in 1986 at the age of 98.

Her historic adobe home and studio in Abiquiu, New Mexico, is open for tours with advance reservations. The home was purchased in 1945 and is located about 60 miles northwest of Santa Fe. You'll get to experience the environment in which she lived and created some of her most famous work. The cottonwood trees in the valley below her studio were the subject of more than two dozen paintings.

TRIVIA

 WHERE DID GEORGIA O'KEEFFE SAY WAS HER FAVORITE PLACE TO BE WHILE PAINTING?

 HER CUSTOMIZED MODEL A FORD!

GEORGIA O'KEEFFE SPENT HER SUMMERS AT THE GHOST RANCH IN ABIQUIU. NEW MEXICO. A GEORGIA O'KEEFFE MUSEUM IS LOCATED IN SANTA FE.

The home was designated a National Historic Landmark in 1998 and is part of the Georgia O'Keeffe Museum.

Her summer home, Rancho de los Burros, is located 12 miles from Abiquiu at Ghost Ranch. The house sits on 12 acres of a 21,000-acre property. While her summer home is not currently open to the public, the ranch does offer several walking tours to view various landscapes that became paintings. The ranch also offers movie location tours, giving visitors the chance to see where films like *Indiana Jones* and *City Slickers* were filmed. The Ghost Ranch is a popular destination for retreats and trail rides.

The ranch has welcomed famous guests like John Wayne and Charles Lindbergh. Scientists who helped develop the nuclear bomb at Los Alamos also spent time here to de-stress. In 1955, the ranch was given to the Presbyterian Church which continues to operate it to this day.

GEORGIA O'KEEFFE
MUSEUM GALLERIES
217 JOHNSON ST..
SANTA FE. NM 87501
OKEEFFEMUSEUM.ORG

GEORGIA O'KEEFFE
VISITORS CENTER
21120 US 84. ABIQUIU. NM 87510

Amelia Earhart

She was America's "Queen of the Air."

Amelia Earhart was born in Atchison, Kansas, in 1897. She took up flying as a hobby and purchased her first airplane, a Kinner Airster. Earhart was employed as a social worker in Boston when she was selected to be the first female passenger on a transatlantic flight. The person who selected her, publisher George Putnam, would become her husband in 1931. She wrote a book about her first flight called *20 Hrs., 40 Min: Our Flight in the Friendship* and was recognized around the world for her accomplishment.

Putnam became Amelia's manager and arranged flights, appearances, and endorsement deals for his wife. He'd also publish two more of her books: *The Fun of It* and *Last Flight*. In 1931, Earhart was elected President of the Ninety-Nines club—an organization of women who were licensed pilots.

Earhart is remembered for her impressive string of historic firsts. She was the first woman to make a solo transatlantic flight in 1932. She was the first person to fly from Hawaii to the American mainland. She was also the first person to fly solo over both the Atlantic and Pacific Oceans.

She was also known for her fashion sense. She developed a popular brand of wrinkle-free dresses, skirts, and outerwear. Her clothing line, called Amelia Earhart Fashions, helped to finance her flying.

Her final and most notable flight began in June of 1937. On July 2, after traveling over 22,000 miles, Earhart vanished along with her navigator Frederick Noonan. To this day, no one knows for sure what

TRIVIA

Q WHAT BRAND OF CIGARETTES WAS AMELIA EARHART A SPOKESPERSON FOR?

Answer LUCKY STRIKE ★ ★ ★ ★ ★ ★ ★

AMELIA EARHART'S LOCKHEED VEGA 5B AIRPLANE ON DISPLAY AT THE NATIONAL AIR AND SPACE MUSEUM.

happened to them though conspiracy theories abound.

The Amelia Earhart Birthplace Museum is located in Atchison, Kansas, in the Amelia Earhart Historical District. The house sits on a bluff overlooking the Missouri River. The two-story house is full of Earhart family photos, trinkets, and furniture.

The Ninety-Nines Museum of Women Pilots in Oklahoma City has a large collection of Amelia Earhart artifacts. You'll see her leather gloves, gifts she was given from around the world, and numerous maps, photographs, and newspaper clippings. The museum focuses on the history of women in aviation.

There are many other museums around the United States dedicated to flight that exhibit artifacts relating to Earhart's career. Most notably the National Air and Space Museum in Washington, D.C., occasionally displays her Lockheed Vega 5B aircraft. It's the plane she used in 1932 to become the first woman to fly nonstop and alone across the Atlantic Ocean.

AMELIA EARHART
BIRTHPLACE MUSEUM
223 N TERRACE ST.,
ATCHISON, KS 66002
AMELIAEARHARTMUSEUM.ORG

MUSEUM OF WOMEN PILOTS
4300 AMELIA EARHART DR., SUITE A,
OKLAHOMA CITY, OK 73159
MUSEUMOFWOMENPILOTS.ORG

Susan B. Anthony

Her outspoken belief in equality for all would benefit women all over America.

In 1820, Susan B. Anthony was born in Adams, Massachusetts. She grew up in a Quaker family which meant that she believed everyone was equal under God. In her 20s, the Anthony family moved to Rochester, New York, where she joined the abolitionist movement. She became an activist and often spoke out against slavery in public. Her family's farm served as a meeting place for anti-slavery activists including Frederick Douglas.

Anthony was best known as a leading voice for the advancement of women's rights in the United States. She became friends with Elizabeth Stanton, and they worked together fighting for equal pay and the right to vote, founding the American Equal Rights Association. They also launched a newspaper called *The Revolution* that helped to spread the idea of equality for women. She traveled across the country, gave lectures, and became an admired public figure. However, not everyone was on board with her cause.

In 1869, Anthony and Stanton founded the National Woman Suffrage Association to push for a constitutional amendment giving women the right to vote. In 1872, Anthony was arrested for voting in that year's presidential election. Her fight for women's rights continued throughout her entire life. In 1905, she met with President Theodore Roosevelt to lobby for the amendment. She died the next year at the age of 86. Her obituary quoted Anthony in her final days: "To think I have had more than 60 years of hard

TRIVIA

Q **HOW MUCH WAS SUSAN B. ANTHONY FINED FOR ILLEGALLY VOTING IN 1872?**

Answer **$100—WHICH SHE NEVER PAID.** ★ ★ ★

struggle for a little liberty, and then to die without it seems so cruel."

Her hard work and dedication were not in vain. In 1920, the 19th Amendment was added to the US Constitution finally giving women the right to vote.

The National Susan B. Anthony Museum & House has been a National Historic Landmark since 1965. She moved into the house with her mother and sister in 1865. She lived here until her death in 1906. Tours are offered daily along with educational programs. Visitors are allowed to walk into the different bedrooms and stand in the parlor where Anthony was arrested for voting in 1872. The museum hosts an annual celebration of the 19th Amendment to the US Constitution that gave women the right to vote.

The childhood home of Susan B. Anthony is located in Battenville, New York, where she lived from the ages of 13–19. A major renovation project to save the home was announced in January 2020. Her birthplace home is open for tours in Adams, Massachusetts.

SUSAN B. ANTHONY BIRTHPLACE
67 EAST RD., ADAMS, MA 01220
SUSANBANTHONYBIRTHPLACE.COM

SUSAN B. ANTHONY MUSEUM & HOME
17 MADISON ST.,
ROCHESTER, NY 14608
SUSANB.ORG

Laura Ingalls Wilder

A pioneer woman became one of the most influential children's authors in America's history.

Laura Ingalls Wilder was an American writer who became famous for her *Little House on the Prairie* series of children's books. The books drew from her experience growing up and moving around the United States as part of a pioneer family. Her stories became even more well-known thanks to the popular *Little House on the Prairie* television series that ran for nine seasons.

She became a teacher at age 15 and was married by the time she turned 18. Her husband Almanzo Wilder is featured in her book *Farmer Boy*. Their marriage was difficult early on because of the death of their baby son, poor crops, a fire, and becoming sick with diphtheria. Laura fully recovered but Almanzo had lingering complications and needed a cane to walk.

Wilder began writing as a way to earn income after the stock market crash of 1929 wiped out all of her investments. She also wanted to preserve her life story, which she did in her first book, an autobiography called *Pioneer Girl*. She started her *Little House* books in 1932 at the age of 65. Her daughter, Rose Wilder Lane, is widely considered responsible for encouraging her mother to write her stories.

Wilder wrote about living in Pepin, Wisconsin; Independence, Kansas; Walnut Grove, Minnesota; Burr Oak, Iowa; and De Smet, South Dakota. Wilder's final stop was in the town of Mansfield,

TRIVIA

> **Q** WHAT ACTOR PORTRAYED LAURA'S FATHER, CHARLES INGALLS, IN THE TELEVISION SERIES *LITTLE HOUSE ON THE PRAIRIE*?
>
> *Answer* **MICHAEL LANDON**

LAURA INGALLS WILDER'S FINAL HOME IN MANSFIELD, MISSOURI, ATTRACTS OVER 30,000 VISITORS A YEAR.

Missouri. Mansfield is approximately 45 miles east of Springfield in the southwest part of the state. Laura Ingalls Wilder lived to be 90 years old.

The farmhouse where Laura and Almanzo lived is now located on the historic Rocky Ridge Farm in Missouri and has remained as it was in 1957. All of the *Little House* books were written by hand on tablets of paper at both the homes situated on Rocky Ridge Farm which attracts about 30,000 visitors a year. Guests have the chance to see the home, her study, and her writing desk the way Laura left them. Displays include Pa's fiddle, pieces of Laura's wedding china, and the wagon they used to make the trip from South Dakota.

The property is open to the public from March–November. There are six other Wilder sites around the United States that offer tours or have museums, but the Rocky Ridge museum contains the most comprehensive of all the Ingalls and Wilder family collections. Links to each destination are made available at: lauraingallswilderhome.com.

LAURA INGALLS WILDER HISTORIC HOME & MUSEUM
3060 HWY. A, MANSFIELD, MISSOURI 65704
LAURAINGALLSWILDERHOME.COM

Mark Twain

He went from pilot on the Missouri riverfront to the Father of American literature.

Samuel Clemens was born in a tiny village called Florida, Missouri. He was the sixth of seven children. At age 4, Clemens moved with his family to an up-and-coming nearby river town called Hannibal. Growing up in Hannibal inspired some of the most beloved stories written under his more famous pen name, Mark Twain. For example, the girl who lived across the street from his parents' house was named Laura Hawkins. She was the inspiration for Becky Thatcher. Tom Blankenship was a childhood friend from a poor local family who inspired the character of Huckleberry Finn.

Twain quit school after his father's death when he was just 12 years old. With the family falling into poverty, he soon went to work for a local newspaper as a typesetter. Later, Twain worked for newspapers in New York and Philadelphia for a short time but returned to Hannibal in 1857 and became a riverboat pilot. In 1861, the Civil War ended his job since river traffic had come to a halt.

He tried his hand at various careers, but writing was his obvious talent. Twain's big break came in 1865 with the publication of a short story called "Jim Smiley and His Jumping Frog." The piece was featured in newspapers across the country. He began writing about his travels with unique tongue-in-cheek observations that became popular with readers. His first book was called *The Innocents Abroad*.

Twain's simple, yet prolific, musings have lasted for generations and continue to be relatable. Some of his most notable adages

Q WHAT WAS THE SEQUEL TO *THE ADVENTURES OF TOM SAWYER?*

Answer **TOM SAWYER ABROAD**

TOURISTS CAN VISIT HANNIBAL, MISSOURI, WHICH INSPIRED MANY OF MARK TWAIN'S STORIES.

include: "If you tell the truth, you don't have to remember anything"; "Wrinkles should merely indicate where the smiles have been"; and "Never argue with stupid people, they will drag you down to their level and beat you with experience."

In 1870, Twain married and started a family in Buffalo, New York, before moving to Hartford, Connecticut. Eventually, the family acquired enough money to move into a beautiful, brand-new home in Hartford where they'd live from 1874–1891.

The three-story, 25-room house is now open for tours and hosts events throughout the year. Guests marvel that, at the time it was built, it had modern innovations like gas lights, hot and cold water, and flushing toilets. One of the bathrooms had a shower which was rare for those days. Another rare feature was the burglar alarm which ran on batteries. While living in the home, Twain published *The Adventures of Tom Sawyer; Old Times on the Mississippi; Sketches, New and Old*; and *A Tramp Abroad*.

The Mark Twain Birthplace State Historic Site in Florida, Missouri, has preserved the two-room cabin where he was born. The site has a handwritten manuscript of *The Adventures of Tom Sawyer* and a selection of furnishings from Twain's Connecticut home.

Curators of Mark Twain's childhood home in Hannibal have worked to preserve the history of his formative years along the Mississippi River. Visitors can start with a walk through the house where he lived which is now a National Historic Landmark.

You will also have the chance to visit the Becky Thatcher House, Huckleberry Finn House, and the J.M. Clemens Justice of the Peace Office, along with a museum gallery and interpretive center. The white fence, made famous by Tom Sawyer, is a wonderful photo opportunity. The historical marker in front notes: "Here stood the board fence which Tom Sawyer persuaded his gang to pay him for the privilege of whitewashing. Tom sat by and saw that it was well done."

Exploring Hannibal will give you a sense of Twain's younger days and the inspiration for many of his stories. You can enjoy a riverboat cruise down the Mississippi River or take a tour of the cave where Twain spent much of his childhood playing. Mark Twain Cave is also known for another well-known visitor: in 1879, Jesse James hid in the cave after a botched robbery attempt.

The Mark Twain Museum in downtown Hannibal features many rare artifacts including Twain's famous white jacket, believed to be the only one still in existence. You'll also see one of his pipes, his writing desk and chair, typewriter, and other personal belongings. The museum houses first editions of his books, more than 60 original letters, and some Normal Rockwell paintings created for special editions of *Tom Sawyer* and *Huck Finn*.

Mark Twain died in 1910 at the age of 74. He is buried at Woodlawn Cemetery in Elmira, New York.

HIS THREE-STORY, 25-ROOM ESTATE IN HARTFORD, CONNECTICUT, WHERE HE LIVED AS AN ADULT IS ALSO OPEN FOR TOURS.

MARK TWAIN BOYHOOD HOME
120 MAIN ST., HANNIBAL, MO 63401
VISITHANNIBAL.COM

THE MARK TWAIN HOUSE & MUSEUM
351 FARMINGTON AVE., HARTFORD, CT 06105
MARKTWAINHOUSE.ORG

Yogi Berra

The son of immigrants becomes a humble hero and sports legend.

Yogi Berra was born and raised in a mostly Italian neighborhood in St. Louis, Missouri, known as The Hill. As a kid, Berra regularly played sandlot baseball with friends and tried out for the St. Louis Cardinals in 1941 at age 16. Instead, he'd wind up with the New York Yankees in their minor league system. World War II was underway and at age 18, Yogi left baseball to join the United States Navy. During the war, he served on the USS *Bayfield* during the Normandy landings.

Berra's first big-league appearance with the New York Yankees came in September of 1946. He would go on to play in 18 seasons with the team. As a player, he holds the record for most appearances in World Series (14) and World Series Championship games (10). He also hit the first pinch-hit home run in World Series history. His number was retired by the Yankees in 1972, the same year he was inducted into the National Baseball Hall of Fame. Berra died in 2015 at the age of 90.

He had a unique way of phrasing things that resulted in oft-quoted sayings which continue to amuse. Some of his favorite quips include: "It ain't over 'til it's over"; "When you come to a fork in the road, take it"; "If you don't know where you're going, you'll end up someplace else"; and "A nickel ain't worth a dime anymore."

The Yogi Berra Museum & Learning Center is located on the campus of Montclair State University. It first opened in 1998 and

Q YOGI BERRA GREW UP IN ST. LOUIS AND LIVED DIRECTLY ACROSS THE STREET FROM WHAT OTHER FUTURE FAMOUS BASEBALL PLAYER?

Answer JOE GARAGIOLA ★ ★ ★ ★ ★

> "You've got to be very careful if you don't know where you're going, because you might not get there."
>
> ‚YOGI BERRA

THE YOGI BERRA MUSEUM IS LOCATED ON THE CAMPUS OF MONTCLAIR STATE UNIVERSITY IN LITTLE FALLS, NEW JERSEY.

continues to focus on sports education and Berra's life. The exhibits share the story of Berra, a son of immigrants, who achieved the American dream and lived a full life on and off the field. Some of the items on display include the glove Berra used to catch during the only perfect game in World Series history, several autographed and "game-used" items, and nine of his championship rings.

The main gallery focuses on topics that were important to Berra: family, community, individualism, and teamwork. A stadium-themed theater shows documentaries and hosts public events and film screenings. An interactive exhibit called *PITCH!* allows guests to face an animated batter and catcher displayed on a video screen. The experience measures the velocity of your throw and the accuracy of the pitch. The intuitive video wall even has a catcher that delivers "Yogi-isms" when appropriate.

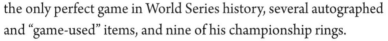

YOGI BERRA MUSEUM & LEARNING CENTER
8 YOGI BERRA DR., LITTLE FALLS, NJ 07424
YOGIBERRAMUSEUM.ORG

Muhammad Ali

"If you even dream of beating me, you better wake up and apologize."

Cassius Clay was born in 1942 in Louisville, Kentucky. His path to greatness began with a stolen bike. When he was 12, Clay told a policer officer he was going to beat up the person who stole it. That police officer, Joe Martin, happened to be a boxing coach and wound up teaching Clay how to box. The boy learned quickly and found that he was faster than other fighters his age. He used his speed to throw fast punches and retreat before they could hit back.

Clay competed in the 1960 Olympics and won a gold medal in light-weight boxing. Upon his return, he was still turned away at an whites-only restaurant. Racial justice was an important cause he worked for his entire life.

As an amateur boxer, Clay won 100 fights and lost only five. Before long, he was considered one of the best light-heavyweight boxers in the world. He became heavyweight champion in 1964 after defeating Sonny Liston. While it wasn't a knockout, Liston refused to fight in the seventh round. As a professional boxer, Clay was known for his "trash talk" where he made up rhymes to annoy his opponent. He routinely referred to himself as "The Greatest." He was also known for his witty and sometimes inspirational sayings. His notable quotes include: "Don't count the days, make the days count" and "Float like a butterfly, sting like a bee."

Clay changed his name to Muhammad Ali after converting to the religion of Islam. His religious and political beliefs created the

TRIVIA

True or False?	MUHAMMAD ALI STARRED IN A BROADWAY PLAY.
Answer	TRUE! IT WAS CALLED *BUCK WHITE* AND IT ONLY LASTED SEVEN PERFORMANCES.

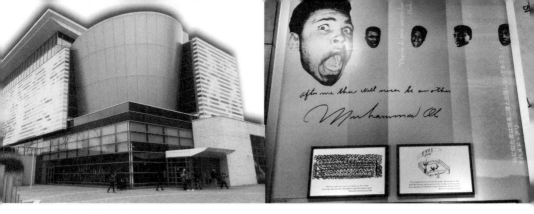

THE MUHAMMAD ALI CENTER IN DOWNTOWN LOUISVILLE, KENTUCKY, OPENED IN 2005 AND TELLS THE STORY OF ALI'S INCREDIBLE LIFE AND CAREER.

controversy which surrounded him for much of his life. He refused to serve in the US Army after being drafted to fight in Vietnam and had his boxing title revoked in 1967. He was convicted for refusing to join the US Army and sentenced to five years in prison. The US Supreme Court reversed his sentence, agreeing that Ali's religious objection to fighting was sincere.

Ali returned to boxing in 1970 with historic matches between Joe Frazier and George Foreman and regained his popularity in the United States. After being diagnosed with Parkinson's disease in the 1980s, he claimed that his outlook on life had changed. He began an endless parade of charity work around the world, using his celebrity status as a means to raise hundreds of millions of dollars. He helped many important causes like Special Olympics, Project A.L.S., UNICEF, and St. Jude Children's Hospital.

In 1999, *Sports Illustrated* named him Sportsman of the Century.

In 2005, he helped found the Muhammad Ali Center in downtown Louisville. The exhibits at the museum and educational center tell the story of a boxing legend who became as famous for his personal beliefs as he was for his fights in the ring. Even if you don't consider yourself a fan of Ali, or boxing in general, it's a worthwhile visit. The center systematically lays out his core thoughts and values in neatly produced displays. Your tour begins with a short documentary before the theater-style doors open up to a wide range of exhibits and interactive displays.

The center focuses heavily on Ali's six core principles:

Confidence: belief in oneself, one's abilities, and one's future.

Conviction: the courage to stand behind a firm belief, despite pressure to do otherwise.

Dedication: the act of devoting all of one's energy, effort, and ability to a certain task.

Giving: to contribute voluntarily without expecting something in return.

Respect: esteem for, or a sense of the worth or excellence of oneself and others.

Spirituality: a sense of awe, reverence, and inner peace.

An oval-shaped exhibit space pays tribute to Ali's boxing career, and around the corner is a regulation-size boxing ring that was used in the movie *Ali* starring Will Smith. Other artifacts include the torch that was used in the Atlanta Olympic Games in 1996 as well as video screens displaying over a dozen of his famous fights. The center regularly provides educational programs and hosts charity events to benefit causes that were important to Ali.

Muhammad Ali died on June 3, 2016. A granite monument above his grave reads: "Service to others is the rent you pay for your room in Heaven." He is buried at Cave Hill Cemetery in Louisville, which is known as the resting place for another famous Louisville resident–Col. Harland Sanders.

MUHAMMAD ALI CENTER
144 N 6TH ST., LOUISVILLE, KY 40202
ALICENTER.ORG

Dwight Eisenhower

From small town Kansas to the front lines of World War II, Eisenhower helped save the world from evil.

Dwight Eisenhower was born in Denison, Texas, and grew up in Abilene, Kansas. He was an accomplished general in the US military, leading Allied forces to victory in World War II. From 1953–1961, he was the 34th president of the United States. His list of career accomplishments is long. He authorized construction of the interstate highway system, founded NASA, and added Alaska and Hawaii as states. He signed two important civil rights bills into law, giving all Americans the right to vote and enforced the desegregation of schools.

The Eisenhower's farm in Gettysburg, Pennsylvania, served as a weekend home and retreat for the president. After leaving office, it became their full-time home. It is one of the more authentic presidential estates because almost everything inside is exactly the way it was when they lived there. These aren't reproductions or replicas of belongings or furnishings; it was the actual property of the Eisenhower family.

Walking through the home, you'd never really know that he was once president of the United States. Sure, there are gifts from world leaders spread around the estate, mainly in the living room where Mrs. Eisenhower liked to welcome special guests. Most of the home is very down-to-earth, including the TV trays that the couple used to eat dinner many nights while Ike flipped through channels on

TRIVIA

Q AS A GENERAL, WHAT DID EISENHOWER INSIST BE DOCUMENTED THROUGH PHOTOS AND FILM?

Answer NAZI CONCENTRATION CAMPS, OUT OF FEAR THAT ONE DAY PEOPLE WOULDN'T BELIEVE IT HAPPENED.

THE CUSTOM PODIUM THAT TRAVELED WITH EISENHOWER WHEN HE GAVE SPEECHES.

his black and white TV in the sunroom. The rangers giving the tours will also point out that, after leaving office, Ike preferred to be called "General" rather than "President."

Mamie Eisenhower's love of all things pink is a sensory overload as you tour the upstairs of the home, especially in the bathroom and bedroom. A quick peek into the closet shows more pink towels and wash cloths than one person should be allowed to own.

The back side of the home has a garden area and a patio where Ike would barbecue. You'll also see a PGA-approved putting green in the back yard. Today, it's still maintained as though the former president could show up at any minute to practice his putting.

Other highlights of the property include the Eisenhower farm, the landing pad for the presidential helicopter (it's just grass), and the barns and garage where you'll find equipment and vehicles used by the family.

Visitors cannot drive directly to the property but instead must book a tour through the Gettysburg Visitors Center and join a tour group that will arrive via shuttle bus. Most of the property, including the house, can then be explored at your own pace. There is a modest fee for the shuttle ride.

The Eisenhower Presidential Library was renovated in 2019 and has the added bonus of being located directly next to his childhood home. Also located on the property is the final resting place of the president and his wife, Mamie. Their graves are located inside a small sanctuary with beautiful stained glass windows. The former president designed it himself and wanted visitors to be able to experience a quiet moment or two during their visit.

Most visitors will only see the museum because each presidential library is in fact a research center where documents related to each president's time in office are stored and organized as part of the National Archives. The Eisenhower Library, for example, has a

EISENHOWER'S CHILDHOOD HOME IN ABILENE, KANSAS

whopping 26 million pages of material. As documents become declassified, the collection grows even bigger. Each presidential library has one-of-a-kind items that you won't see anywhere else, like the microphone Eisenhower used at press conferences or the custom-built podium that traveled with him on official trips. They even have the engagement ring he gave to the former First Lady.

Kids will be stunned to learn what "modern technology" looked like during the years Eisenhower was in office. In the late 1950s a state-of-the-art communications phone looks like something you'd see at a garage sale. Typewriters? What are those? And history buffs will be intrigued to see stationery that belonged to none other than Adolf Hitler along with the actual D-Day planning table. Car lovers will get a kick out of the Eisenhowers' 1914 electric Rauch and Lang automobile that once belonged to Mamie's mother.

Outside is a statue of the former president and general that stands 11 feet tall. It's a lasting memorial to a great American hero and one of the most popular and well-respected leaders in history.

EISENHOWER PRESIDENTIAL LIBRARY AND CHILDHOOD HOME
200 SE 4TH ST., ABILENE, KS 67410
EISENHOWERLIBRARY.GOV

GETTYSBURG VISITORS CENTER (FOR EISENHOWER FARM TOURS)
1195 BALTIMORE PIKE, GETTYSBURG, PA 17325
NPS.GOV/GETT

EISENHOWER BIRTHPLACE & MUSEUM
609 S LAMAR AVE., DENISON, TX 75021
THC.TEXAS.GOV

MADE IN THE USA

FOOD & DRINK

★ FINDING THE AMERICAN DREAM ★

Milton Hershey

He never gave up and became America's Candy Man.

Milton Hershey became interested in developing candy in his early teens. After learning the trade from a confectioner in Lancaster, Pennsylvania, he set his sights on opening his first candy shop. For five years, Hershey operated a small store in Philadelphia, but it was never the success he imagined.

Hershey would launch two other businesses after his discovery of caramel but both ventures failed. In 1883, he finally found success with the Lancaster Caramel Company whose products were in demand all over the country. Hershey sold the company in 1900 for $1 million—a staggering amount of money at the time. Not bad for a guy who only had a fourth-grade education.

His newest business, The Hershey Chocolate Company took off beyond his wildest dreams when Hershey figured out how to mass produce and distribute milk chocolate candy. The original Hershey Bar debuted in 1900. In 1907, Hershey had developed another signature candy called the Hershey Kiss.

During the Great Depression, demand for candy dropped significantly, but Hershey kept his employees working. Instead of producing chocolate, however, they helped build a new hotel that would sit on Pat's Hill, overlooking the company's headquarters.

In 1909, Hershey opened a private school specifically for low-income children. Milton and his wife Catherine loved children but

TRIVIA

Q HOW BIG WAS THE LARGEST PIECE OF HERSHEY'S CHOCOLATE?

Answer IN 2007, HERSHEY MADE A 12-FOOT TALL, 30,000-POUND KISS, WRAPPED IN 16,000 FEET OF FOIL.

were unable to have any of their own. This seemed like a good way for them to give back to their community and help the young people who needed it most. The Milton Hershey School still provides tuition-free education through grade 12 to qualifying students. In 1918, Hershey gave his entire fortune to the school.

HERSHEY

Model industrial town and noted tourism destination established in 1903 and named for its founder, Milton S. Hershey (1857-1945). Hershey's companies developed housing, recreation, education, and cultural facilities, financial institutions, public utilities, a transit system, and the world's largest chocolate factory that opened in June, 1905.

PENNSYLVANIA HISTORICAL AND MUSEUM COMMISSION   2003

Milton Hershey died in 1945 at the age of 88, though it could have been sooner. Hershey had purchased tickets for a trip on board the *Titanic*. Days before they were to leave, his travel plans changed because of business concerns.

Today, the company he founded has more than 15,000 employees with products sold in more than 60 countries. Its most popular candy is Reese's Peanut Butter Cups. Other products owned by Hershey include Almond Joy, Kit Kat, Whoppers, York Peppermint Patties, and Milk Duds.

The town of Hershey, Pennsylvania, originally built for employees of the Hershey Company, bills itself as "the sweetest place on earth." That's because it is! The first thing you're likely to notice is that each light pole in town is topped with a giant Hershey Kiss. Today, there are so many wonderful attractions and experiences that you'll need to set aside several days to enjoy all of them.

If you're looking for amusement, Hershey Park is a first-class theme park with 15 roller coasters and other fun rides for all ages. Another must-do experience is Hershey's Chocolate World. Here you'll find the world's biggest Hershey gift shop. From peanut butter cups that are the size of your head to specialty items you won't find anywhere else, this place is particularly dangerous for chocolate lovers.

Of course, at every Hershey experience around town, they feed you complimentary chocolate. You'll have it waiting for you when you check into the Hershey Lodge or the historic Hotel Hershey. You'll be given pieces of chocolate when you take their free simulated factory tour. (It's not really a tour of the factory but more of an amusement ride that takes you through the production process.)

You can make your own candy bar or even take a class on chocolate tasting. You'll definitely want to hop on the trolley and get a narrated tour of the town. You will pass by the mansion where Milton Hershey lived although the home isn't typically open for public tours. You'll also pass by Hershey Gardens which opened in 1937. The facility has grown in size to 23 acres from its original three and a half when Mr. Hershey requested "a nice garden of roses." The rose garden is still intact, and the entire property is open to the public.

For an up-close history lesson on Milton Hershey and the entire Hershey company, consider visiting The Hershey Story. This biographical museum tells the tale of a man who worked hard, never gave up, and—upon becoming successful—didn't forget the people who helped him along the way. In addition to advertising campaigns and old promotional items, you'll see the machine that wraps those delicious Hershey Kisses!

HERSHEYPA.COM

THE HERSHEY STORY MUSEUM INCLUDES INTERESTING EXHIBITS LIKE THE MACHINE THAT MAKES AND WRAPS HERSHEY KISSES CANDY.

Charles Alderton

The man from Waco, Texas, creates America's first major soft drink.

In the late 1800s, Charles Alderton was a pharmacist at Morrison's Old Corner Drug Store in Waco, Texas. The drug store, owned by a man named Wade Morrison, included a soda fountain where patrons had their choice of various flavors mixed with carbonated water.

Alderton was known to experiment with soda recipes, even keeping a journal of his ideas. He loved the smell of the drug store, which typically had a variety of flavorful scents that would linger throughout the day. He decided to create a recipe that would taste similar to that smell. After many experiments and taste tests, he finally found the perfect mix. His concoction included 23 different flavors and was known to locals as The Waco.

To say it was popular would be an understatement. Not only was it loved by his own customers, word was spreading around town to other soda fountain operators about this tasty, unique creation. It wasn't long before they wanted the syrup mixture to sell in their own stores. Demand grew so fast that Alderton and Morrison could no longer continue business as usual in their current building.

Plans to expand production were taking shape and Alderton decided to sell his recipe to Morrison and stick with a career in pharmacy. Morrison then teamed up with an established beverage producer in Waco named Robert Lazenby. Lazenby already had experience in production at his own large facility that was making

TRIVIA

Q IN THE DR PEPPER AD CAMPAIGNS, WHAT SPECIFIC TIMES WERE SUPPOSEDLY BEST FOR ENJOYING THE SOFT DRINK?

Answer ACCORDING TO THE COMPANY'S RESEARCH: 10 A.M., 2 P.M., AND 4 P.M. WERE THE TIMES OUR BODY MOST NEEDED A BOOST OF ENERGY

THE MUSEUM IS LOCATED IN THE 1906 BOTTLING PLANT THAT STILL INCLUDES THE ORIGINAL WATER WELL THAT WAS USED TO MAKE DR PEPPER.

Circle "A" Ginger Ale. Morrison's beverage was produced on a larger scale in the new building and work had begun to expand the product beyond Waco and Texas.

The drink debuted to the masses for the first time at the 1904 World's Fair in St. Louis, Missouri. By then, consumers knew the creation by its new name: Dr Pepper. While nobody knows for certain why Morrison chose the name, one thing is for sure: Charles Alderton's mixture was a hit—and still is.

The creative idea of one small-town Texas pharmacist led to over 20 manufacturing and bottling facilities in North America along with more than 100 warehouses and distribution centers. Dr Pepper Snapple Group employs more than 21,000 American workers and owns more than 50 brands of refreshments including 7 Up, A&W, and Hawaiian Punch. The company earned more than $6.7 billion in 2017.

The Dr Pepper Museum in Waco is housed in the original 1906 bottling plant. You'll see a wide variety of company artifacts and exhibits including the original water well that was used for production.

DR PEPPER MUSEUM
300 S 5TH ST., WACO, TEXAS 76701

Dan & Frank Carney

Kansas brothers take a chance and launch America's first pizza restaurant chain.

In the summer of 1958, Dan and Frank Carney opened a small pizza shop with the help of a $600 loan from their mother. Using secondhand equipment, the Carney brothers converted a 500-square-foot bar into the world's first Pizza Hut restaurant in Wichita, Kansas. On opening night, the brothers gave away free pizza to drum up publicity for their new venture.

Though the early days were chaotic, the brothers soon found their footing. In 1959, they franchised a second location in Topeka. A year later, a third location opened in the town of Aggieville. Within 10 years, Pizza Hut had grown to 300 locations.

The original store was preserved and moved to the campus of Wichita State University. In 2018, it was transformed into The Pizza Hut Museum and its location is fitting considering it is now part of Wichita State's "innovation campus." The brick building, also known as Store #1, serves as inspiration to students with big ideas and dreams of their own.

Inside the museum are video presentations that feature personal stories from the Carney brothers about opening their first location. Another video features a former CEO sharing the growing pains of the company. A third exhibit plays the first Pizza Hut commercial jingle.

Some of the featured artifacts include menus from various locations around the world and a hand-written recipe for their pizza sauce. One display case highlights the popular children's reading program "Book-

TRIVIA

Q WHAT FAMOUS NFL HEAD COACH ONCE MANAGED A PIZZA HUT IN WICHITA?

Answer **BILL PARCELLS** ★ ★ ★ ★ ★ ★

THE PIZZA HUT MUSEUM IS LOCATED ON THE CAMPUS OF WICHITA STATE UNIVERSITY AND IS FREE TO THE PUBLIC.

It" that rewarded grade school kids with a free pizza for reading a certain number of books.

Among the interesting stories told in The Pizza Hut Museum is how the franchise stores got their iconic "hut" shaped roofing. The proposed $30,000 cost for designing those instantly recognizable buildings was too steep for the Carney brothers. The counteroffer for the design was $100 for each location as it opened. That agreement wound up earning the architect over $1,000,000.

So, where did the name Pizza Hut come from? Turns out, the exterior sign above the door fit nine characters. The brothers knew they wanted the word "pizza" in their shop name which left them three characters to spare. The building looked like a hut so that's what they called it. After successfully becoming the largest pizza chain in the world, the brothers sold their company to PepsiCo in 1977.

Dan Carney left the business to become a venture capitalist and work with local charities around Wichita. Frank went on to help found another pizza chain—Papa Johns.

THE PIZZA HUT MUSEUM
2090 INNOVATION BLVD., WICHITA, KS 67208
WICHITA.EDU/MUSEUMS/PIZZAHUTMUSEUM

Richard & Maurice McDonald

A small California restaurant started a new concept: fast food.

Richard and Maurice "Mac" McDonald moved to Southern California from New England hoping to find success in the movie business. They did not. Instead, they focused their attention on developing a concept where restaurants served customers quickly with reasonably priced meals.

The McDonald brothers' first business venture was a hot dog stand in 1937. The stand, located in Monrovia, California, served patrons near a local racetrack. Once racing season ended, the duo had very few customers. They decided to open up a barbecue restaurant 50 miles away in San Bernardino. Their new restaurant became a hit, especially with younger people and families looking for a cheap meal. The food was served to patrons in their vehicles by young ladies known as carhops.

Over time, the McDonald brothers had studied and devised a new business plan that would maximize profits and speed up service. They shut down their San Bernardino store, despite its popularity, and reopened three months later. The new McDonald's featured a walk-up counter for orders, a redesigned kitchen to maximize food assembly, and a new menu. The limited items for sale now included hamburgers, cheeseburgers, soft drinks, milk, coffee, potato chips,

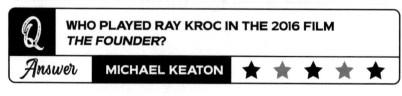

TRIVIA

Q WHO PLAYED RAY KROC IN THE 2016 FILM *THE FOUNDER?*

Answer **MICHAEL KEATON** ★ ★ ★ ★ ★

and apple pie. French fries soon replaced the chips and milk shakes were also added.

The brothers began to franchise their restaurants in 1953. The new locations included the same assembly line set-up, known as the Speedee Service System, along with the now iconic golden arches out in front. They had eight operating locations by the time they met Ray Kroc. Kroc, who sold mixing machines for a living, became fascinated with the business plan the McDonald brothers had invented.

In 1954, Ray Kroc took charge of opening new McDonald's restaurants across the country with his first new store in the town of Des Plaines, Illinois. Kroc was both ambitious and brilliant, determined to open at least 1,000 new restaurants. He demanded that each new location follow the same procedures for making food and maintain a high level of customer service and cleanliness. He eventually bought out the McDonald brothers, netting each of them $1 million. By the time of Kroc's death in 1984, McDonald's had opened more than 7,500 locations. As of 2020, there were nearly 38,000.

As the restaurants expanded across the country, so did the menu. In 1965, the Filet-O-Fish sandwich was added at the suggestion of a franchise owner in Cincinnati where there was a large Catholic community. A Pittsburgh franchise owner developed a sandwich in 1968 called the Big Mac. In the 1970s, McDonald's debuted the

Quarter Pounder and Egg McMuffin. Chicken McNuggets were added in 1983.

In 1975, the company founded Ronald McDonald House in Philadelphia. There are currently hundreds of locations across the globe with the mission of keeping families together when travel is a must for the care of a sick child. No eligible family is ever turned away.

Located along historic Route 66 in San Bernardino, California, is the Original McDonald's Museum. While the original building is no longer standing, it is the actual site of the first restaurant opened by the McDonald brothers. This was the spot where they debuted their revolutionary Speedee Service System in 1948.

Inside the museum is a treasure trove of McDonald's memorabilia including original menus, kitchen equipment, and pieces of flooring. You'll even see the original mixer that was sold to the restaurant by Ray Kroc. The collection of exhibits includes display cases full of McDonald's signs, promotional items, packaging, and Ronald McDonald dolls. Fans from around the world have donated toys to show what children in other countries get with their Happy Meals. The large sign out front and classic children's playground pieces are sure to bring back memories.

Unfortunately, the neighborhood has changed a lot since the 1940s and you'll want to be aware of your surroundings if you plan to visit. Locals say it's safe to visit during the day, but always be smart!

The oldest operating McDonald's is located about an hour west in the town of Downey. The sign out front features the original McDonald's mascot, Speedee, which was designed and portrayed by long-time *Today Show* personality, Willard Scott. (Speedee was replaced by Ronald McDonald in 1967.) The Downey location has a small museum with memorabilia and is the only McDonald's store that still sells fried apple pies.

ORIGINAL MCDONALD'S MUSEUM
1398 NE. ST.. SAN BERNARDINO. CA 92405

OLDEST OPERATING MCDONALD'S RESTAURANT & MUSEUM
10207 LAKEWOOD BLVD.. DOWNEY. CA 90240

THE OLDEST OPERATING MCDONALD'S IS IN DOWNEY. CALIFORNIA. THE RESTAURANT. WHICH OPENED IN 1953. FEATURES A SMALL MUSEUM AND IS LOCATED AN HOUR WEST OF SAN BERNARDINO—SITE OF THE FIRST MCDONALD'S STORE.

Adolphus Busch

A German immigrant became America's King of Beers.

In 1839, Adolphus Busch was born in Heese, Germany. He was one of 22 children. His parents ran a business providing supplies to wineries and breweries. At age 18, Busch and three of his brothers moved to the United States and settled in St. Louis, Missouri. Busch served in the Union Army for six months during the American Civil War. It was during this time that he learned that his father had died and left him a portion of his estate.

Returning to St. Louis after the Civil War, Busch entered the brewery business. His wife's father was named Eberhard Anheuser. Anheuser purchased the Bavarian Brewery after it had fallen into bankruptcy. Busch began working with his father-in-law in 1864. The company began to grow and soon dominated beer production in the region. In 1879 the company changed its name to Anheuser-Busch.

Anheuser died in 1880 and Busch became president of the company. Continued success made Busch a very wealthy man. He owned mansions in California, New York, and a main residence in St. Louis. A personal railcar named Adolphus transported him to destinations all over the country. He also contributed millions of dollars to charitable causes.

While president of Anheuser-Busch, he oversaw innovation and grew the company's brand to new markets all over the United States. One of his most notable innovations was the introduction of refrigerated freight cars. Busch ran the company for over 30 years

TRIVIA

Q THE ORIGINAL CLYDESDALES WERE A GIFT TO AUGUST BUSCH TO CELEBRATE WHAT?

Answer | **THE END OF PROHIBITION** |

before he passed away and his son, August A. Busch, Sr. took the reins in 1913.

The oldest and largest brewery site is located in the historic Soulard neighborhood of St. Louis. Its location was chosen based on access to the Mississippi River and the large presence of German immigrants in the 1800s. Tours of the facility have been given since 1904. The Budweiser Brewery Experience is a free walking tour that lasts about an hour. You'll see the Brew House and Budweiser Clydesdale stables. You'll end your tour in the biergarten where you're given a free sample.

The brewery offers two additional fee-based tours that give expanded looks behind the scenes. The Day Fresh Tour adds a look at the packaging plant and beechwood aging cellars. Visitors will also leave with a bottle of beer that was produced on the day of their visit. The most expensive tour option is a Beermaster Tour which includes a look at the finishing cellars and allows you to sample beer directly from a finishing tank.

The Budweiser Clydesdales are also based in St. Louis. They can be found at Grant's Farm, less than 10 miles from the brewery. The Clydesdales are housed in various stables on the property and are often seen roaming around in the open field across the street. Grant's Farm is an animal reserve and event space that is free and open to the public. They offer animal shows, interactive experiences, and a bauernhof which is German for farmstead. The Bauernhof was built in 1913 and currently houses the Busch family's historic carriage collection. The farm was once owned by Ulysses S. Grant and the log cabin he built in 1856 is still standing. Grant's home, White Haven, is next door and open for tours through the National Park Service.

The Busch family also maintains a mansion on the site though it's not generally open to the public.

There are other sites around the United States where visitors can experience Budweiser tours and see the world-famous Clydesdales. There are smaller breweries located in Fort Collins, Colorado, and Merrimack, New Hampshire. You can also tour Warm Springs Ranch, the facility responsible for breeding the Clydesdales. Tours must be booked in advance through their website.

Busch invested in other businesses and real estate throughout his life, particularly in Dallas, Texas, which was becoming a major city in the early 20th century. One investment was the Adolphus Hotel in downtown Dallas. When constructed, it was the tallest building in the state of Texas. The hotel was a personal project for Busch who wanted to create the most lavish, posh hotel in the city. The Adolphus Hotel has hosted many celebrities and dignitaries including Queen Elizabeth, George H. W. Bush, and Bob Hope. It is listed on the National Register of Historic Places.

Adolphus Busch is laid to rest at Bellefontaine Cemetery in St. Louis.

WARM SPRINGS RANCH
25270 STATE HWY. 98, BOONEVILLE, MO 65233
WARMSPRINGSRANCH.COM

GRANT'S FARM
10501 GRAVOIS RD., ST. LOUIS, MO 63123
GRANTSFARM.COM

BUDWEISER BREWERY EXPERIENCE
12TH AND LYNCH ST., ST. LOUIS, MO 63118
BUDWEISERTOURS.COM

ANHEUSER-BUSCH WELCOMES TRAVELERS TO ITS MAIN HEADQUARTERS, AS WELL AS GRANT'S FARM, BOTH LOCATED IN ST. LOUIS, MISSOURI.

Edmund McIlhenny

In the midst of financial ruin, he created what would be the world's most popular hot sauce.

Edmund McIlhenny was 22 when he moved to Louisiana from his hometown in Maryland. He married Mary Avery in 1859. After the Civil War, in financial ruin, McIlhenny went to live with his in-laws in a plantation house on Avery Island. He worked in the gardens and grew a variety of fruits and vegetables.

He obtained some hot pepper seeds and began to experiment with pepper sauces. By 1870, he had received a patent for his creation of Tabasco, named after a state in Mexico. McIlhenny didn't seem to realize the potential of the product he had created. Future generations of the family expanded the sale of Tabasco and developed it into the household name it is today.

It takes nearly five years for the entire production process to be completed. All of the pepper seeds still originate on Avery Island. The peppers are still handpicked in the same manner they were by McIlhenny. The Tabasco factory produces 700,000 bottles each day. In case you were wondering, a 2 ounce bottle of original Tabasco contains 720 drops of the hot sauce. The ingredients have always remained the same: tabasco peppers, salt, and high-quality vinegar.

The Tabasco factory is open for tours on Avery Island in Louisiana. The tour runs about 30 minutes and includes views of the various production areas. Be sure to note the sign that indicates how many Tabasco bottles they've produced for the day. You'll see a short video about the McIlhenny family's history and

 IN THE EARLY DAYS OF TABASCO, WHAT WAS USED TO DISTRIBUTE THE HOT SAUCE?

Answer | **DISCARDED COLOGNE BOTTLES**

TABASCO® Pepper Sauce
BOTTLES PRODUCED TODAY

233110

THE PUBLIC CAN TOUR THE FACTORY WHERE TABASCO SAUCE IS PRODUCED AS WELL AS A TABASCO HISTORY MUSEUM ON AVERY ISLAND, LOUISIANA.

see a museum with some company artifacts. Don't miss a great photo opportunity with the larger-than-life bottles of Tabasco. You'll be gifted with some complimentary mini bottles of the spicy sauce at the conclusion of the tour. If that's not enough, a huge gift shop next door is loaded with Tabasco products and merchandise.

The real treat is getting to explore the Jungle Gardens. In the 1890s, McIlhenny preserved 170 acres of the island which is home to thousands of snowy white egrets that return each spring. It's also home to other wildlife including bears, alligators, wildcats, coyotes, and deer. You'll see exotic plants, beautiful Spanish moss, and swamps. Visitors are allowed to take a self-guided driving tour. A mobile phone app is available to enhance your experience.

You can also grab lunch at their on-site restaurant 1868 which offers authentic Cajun favorites and a Bloody Mary bar.

AVERY ISLAND: HOME OF TABASCO
HWY. 329, AVERY ISLAND, LA 70513
TABASCO.COM

Jack Daniel

His product was so good, Frank Sinatra was buried with it.

Jack Daniel was born in 1849 and was the youngest of 10 children. After his father died during the Civil War, he ran away from home. A preacher and moonshine distiller named Dan Lay took the teenager in. Lay and an enslaved man named Nathan "Nearest" Green taught Daniel the process of making whiskey.

In 1866, Daniel opened his own distillery in Lynchburg, Tennessee. In 1904, Jack Daniel's brand won a gold medal at the World's Fair in 1904 for "finest whiskey." That win prompted a surge of interest in Old No. 7, the distillery's premiere product. In 1907, failing health caused Daniel to hand the reins of the operation over to two of his nephews.

One popular tale is that Daniel died from blood poisoning after kicking the office safe to which he often forgot the combination. The story goes that he injured his foot and it became infected, leading to his death. However, Peter Krass, who wrote the biography *Blood and Whiskey: The Life and Times of Jack Daniel* says that particular legend is not true.

Jack Daniel's offers several tours of its Lynchburg distillery. The general tour lasts about 90 minutes. Wear comfortable shoes and dress for the weather because you'll be walking a lot, mostly outdoors.

First, you'll take a bus ride to one of the 87 warehouses on-site. Next up, it's the rickyard where they burn Jack Daniel's sprayed sugar-maple wood until it becomes charcoal. This is the charcoal

Q HOW TALL WAS JACK DANIEL?
Answer ONLY 5 FOOT 2 INCHES! ★ ★ ★ ★

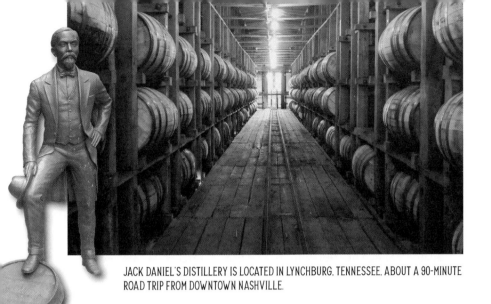

JACK DANIEL'S DISTILLERY IS LOCATED IN LYNCHBURG, TENNESSEE, ABOUT A 90-MINUTE ROAD TRIP FROM DOWNTOWN NASHVILLE.

that is ground down for use in the filtration process—the thing that separates Jack Daniel's Tennessee whiskey from other whiskeys and bourbons.

A natural spring that flows through a limestone cave was one of the reasons Daniel chose to put his distillery in Lynchburg. You'll see that as well as Jack's office and the infamous safe. Then, it's off to visit the still house. Inside there are over 100,000 gallons of mash fermenting at any given moment. From there, you'll see how the process works. As the whiskey drops through the 10-foot-high filtration tank, any remaining impurities are removed. Its final destination is one of the barrels from which the finished whiskey will eventually be poured into bottles for sale.

Oddly enough, Lynchburg is located in a dry county which means you can't purchase most Jack Daniel's products on-site. One way around the law is the sale of "collectible" bottles which you can buy in the gift shop.

JACK DANIEL'S DISTILLERY
133 LYNCHBURG HWY., LYNCHBURG, TN 37352
JACKDANIELS.COM

Otto Frederick Rohwedder

This was the guy responsible for "the greatest thing."

Otto Rohwedder was born and raised in Davenport, Iowa. He graduated college in 1900 and moved to the northwest Missouri town of St. Joseph where he became a jeweler. He operated three jewelry stores where his work with watches sparked an interest in inventing new machines.

Rohwedder had tinkered with an idea for a machine that could slice and then bag loaves of bread, but his blueprints and the prototype were destroyed in a fire in 1917. It took nearly a decade to raise enough money to start all over. By 1927, he had finalized his invention and received a patent for the world's first bread-slicing machine.

In 1928, the first machine was sold to a bakery store owner and friend of Rohwedder in Chillicothe. The presliced loaves of bread became a huge hit with customers at the Chillicothe Baking Company. Store owner Frank Bench claimed his bread sales shot up over 2,000 percent in the first two weeks.

Orders started streaming in for the new machines and sliced bread was here to stay. Sadly, Rohwedder was forced to sell his patents in 1933 in order to avoid financial ruin during the Great Depression.

However, his legacy continued as sliced bread became the norm for American households. Wonder Bread was the first major national brand to sell its bread in sliced form. Rohwedder's slicer

CHILLICOTHE, MISSOURI, IS KNOWN AS THE HOME OF SLICED BREAD. ONE OF THE ORIGINAL BREAD-SLICING MACHINES IS ON DISPLAY IN THE TOWN'S LOCAL HISTORY MUSEUM.

inadvertently helped boost another struggling invention, the automated pop-up toaster. With evenly sliced bread readily available, inventor Charles Strite saw increased demand for his machines that had debuted in 1921.

One of Rohwedder's large, 1,000-pound slicing machines is on display at the Grand River Historical Society Museum in Chillicothe, Missouri. The model on display was sold to Korn's Bakery in Davenport, Iowa, in late 1928. It was the second machine ever used. (The first machine, which was used in Chillicothe, fell apart after about six months of continuous use.) The exhibit is technically on loan from the Smithsonian American History Museum. However, its current location in the town that bills itself The Home of Sliced Bread seems ideal.

While you're visiting Chillicothe be sure to take time and enjoy all of the beautiful murals around town. Each mural is historical in nature, telling different parts of the town's story.

GRAND RIVER HISTORICAL SOCIETY MUSEUM
1401 FOREST DR., CHILLICOTHE, MO 61523
CHILLICOTHEHISTORICAL.ORG

George A. Hormel

A pioneer in the world of food production, he created a comestible people either love or hate.

In 1891, George A. Hormel established Hormel & Co. in Austin, Minnesota. Hormel had worked in a packinghouse when he was just 12 years old and always dreamed of becoming a meat packer. His company became one of the largest food producers in the world and now its products include bacon, sausage, packaged lunch meats, and brands like Dinty Moore beef stew, and Skippy peanut butter.

It was 1937 when Hormel's most notable product made its debut. SPAM, a canned meat known for its long shelf life, became popular during World War II. With the difficulty of delivering fresh meat to troops during combat, Hormel provided an easier alternative with SPAM. SPAM has six simple ingredients: pork (shoulder and ham), salt, water, sugar, potato starch, and sodium nitrite.

Most seem to either love it or hate it when it comes to SPAM. As of 2020, more than eight billion cans have been sold. Hormel claims to process 20,000 pigs a day to keep up with demand. Its popularity tends to fluctuate with the state of the economy. During the Great Recession of 2008, demand for SPAM increased more than 10 percent. In certain parts of the world SPAM is considered a routine staple. According to a study from National Geographic, Hawaii consumes five million pounds of it each year, more than any other US state.

In 2016, Hormel Foods opened a new SPAM museum in downtown Austin. There are seven galleries with various exhibits. Can Central highlights a wide range of fun facts relating to their

THE SPAM MUSEUM IN AUSTIN, MINNESOTA, OFFERS FREE ADMISSION AND TELLS THE STORY OF HORMEL FOODS AND ITS MOST FAMOUS PRODUCT, SPAM.

products while in the World Market gallery, visitors can learn about advertising and SPAM recipes from around the world. There's also a World War II gallery that educates guests on how SPAM helped to keep American troops fed during combat. The museum is 14,000 square feet and includes interactive games, videos, and family friendly activities. For example, visitors can see how tall they are in measurements of SPAM cans.

The museum's gift shop has everything you could possibly think of adorned with the SPAM logo. T-shirts, buttons, lunch boxes, key chains, clocks, and even beach towels promote Hormel's famous product. Of course, you can also purchase any of the actual SPAM products. Admission to the SPAM museum is free.

George Hormel's historic house in Austin is also open for free tours. He and his wife Lillian lived there from 1901 to 1927 before retiring in Southern California.

SPAM MUSEUM
101 3RD AVE.,
AUSTIN, MN 55912
SPAM.COM

HORMEL ESTATE
208 4TH AVE. NW,
AUSTIN, MN 55912
HORMELHISTORICHOME.ORG

Harland Sanders

America's king of fried chicken is proof that you're never too old to dream.

By the time Harland Sanders was in first grade, he was already honing his skills in the kitchen. He had lost his father at age five and shortly afterwards helped take care of his two younger siblings while his mother worked at a local tomato cannery. By the age of seven, Sanders was often making family meals and became skilled in baking bread and cooking vegetables.

His mother remarried in 1902 and Sanders had a rough relationship with his new stepfather. About a year later, he dropped out of the seventh grade and went to live and work on a nearby farm. This began a long run of odd jobs that included painting horse carriages, conducting street cars, working for a blacksmith, and servicing trains. He later studied law and wound up opening his own practice in Little Rock, Arkansas, for a short time.

During his life, Sanders battled with a short temper. He once brawled with one of his own clients in the middle of a courtroom which cost him his law practice. He also was known for using foul language particularly when employees weren't living up to his high standards.

Leading up to World War II, Sanders had been working at a Shell station in Corbin, Kentucky. He started serving meals to customers who stopped for fuel. He became popular locally for his delicious country ham and steaks. Eventually word of his cooking talent

Q **WHY DID COLONEL SANDERS ALWAYS WEAR A WHITE SUIT?**

Answer **TO EASILY HIDE FLOUR STAINS AND TO MATCH HIS WHITE HAIR!**

AN ORIGINAL TUB OF COL. SANDER'S
CHICKEN SEASONING.

spread around the United States after being featured in a food critic's national travel guide. He'd go on to open his own restaurant called Sanders Cafe.

In 1935, Kentucky's governor named Sanders an honorary Colonel "in recognition of his contributions to the state's cuisine." From that point on, he referred to himself as Colonel Sanders.

Sanders traveled the country to sell his mix of herbs and spices. He would often sleep in the back of his car. If a restaurant agreed to use his recipe, they would pay four cents per piece of chicken sold. By 1964, the franchise of Kentucky Fried Chicken locations had grown to more than 600. In 2020, KFC reportedly had over 23,000 stores making it the second-largest fast-food chain in the world.

Travelers can still dine in the old Sanders Cafe in Corbin, Kentucky. A historical marker outside notes its location as the "birthplace of Kentucky Fried Chicken." (Technically that honor goes to a restaurant in Utah, although Sanders Cafe is where the secret recipe and concept actually began.)

Once inside the building you'll see Colonel Sanders's office and the restaurant kitchen, which was purposely designed to be open and viewable by patrons. According to the museum, he wanted the public to see the food being prepared. The all-white design of the kitchen was chosen to quickly spot spills or mess—Sanders was apparently a neat freak and liked things squeaky clean.

It was in this kitchen where he developed the art of pressure-cooking the chicken, which reduced wait times from 35 minutes to just nine minutes for a fresh meal. On the other side of the building, there's an actual KFC location. Near the ordering counter is a small display of memorabilia relating to the early days of the fast-food chain. The museum includes a couple of statues, old business cards, a tub that once contained the secret recipe mix, and various photos and autographs. While not a huge display, it's definitely worth checking out if you're in the area.

The odd part of the restaurant is the model of a motel room which literally sits inside the dining area. Apparently, Sanders purchased a motel across the street and used his restaurant as a way to advertise it. His thinking was that if travelers passing through saw a nice, clean room while grabbing a bite to eat, they would be encouraged to stay in town.

So, what are the secret herbs and spices that are used to make Kentucky Fried Chicken? The original recipe is under lock and key in a vault in Louisville. In fact, today the mixture is still produced in two different locations to keep it secure.

Sanders died in 1980 and was laid to rest at Cave Hill Cemetery* in Louisville, Kentucky. A yellow line on the road leads visitors to the tombstone. It's not uncommon to see flowers and buckets of chicken on the ground.

SANDERS DESIGNED HIS CAFE SO PATRONS COULD EASILY SEE INSIDE THE CLEAN KITCHEN.

SANDERS CAFE 688
HWY. 25 CORBIN, KY 40701

HARLAND SANDERS GRAVE
CAVE HILL CEMETERY
701 BAXTER AVE., LOUISVILLE, KY 40204
*A YELLOW LINE ON THE ROAD LEADS TO SANDERS'S GRAVE.

MADE IN THE USA

HUMBLE BEGINNINGS & HOMES

★ FINDING THE AMERICAN DREAM ★

Ronald Reagan

The 40th president of the United States grew up in Dixon, Illinois, from ages 9 to 22 starting in 1920. The Queen Anne style house where Reagan and his family lived is open for tours from April–October.

816 S HENNEPIN AVE., DIXON, IL 61021
REAGANHOME.ORG

TRIVIA

Q WHAT CANDY DID RONALD REAGAN ALWAYS HAVE IN CLOSE PROXIMITY, INCLUDING ON HIS DESK IN THE OVAL OFFICE?

Answer JELLY BEANS. HE REPORTEDLY STARTED EATING THESE TO KICK A SMOKING HABIT IN 1967.

Bill Clinton

The 42nd president of the United States was born in Hope, Arkansas, and lived in this house with his widowed mother and her parents until the age of four. Clinton grew up to become the Governor of Arkansas and the first "baby boomer" president. The house is maintained by the National Park Service and offers tours throughout the year.

117 S HERVEY ST., HOPE, AR. 71801

CLINTONCHILDHOODHOMEMUSEUM.COM

TRIVIA

Q WHAT OTHER FORMER ARKANSAS GOVERNOR TURNED TELEVISION PERSONALITY WAS RAISED IN HOPE, ARKANSAS?

Answer **MIKE HUCKABEE** ★ ☆ ★ ☆ ★

Bob Dylan

Legendary songwriter, musician, and artist Bob Dylan lived in this home in Hibbing, Minnesota, starting at age six. He lived here from 1948 until he finished high school in 1959. You'll recognize it by the Bob Dylan Drive sign on the street. It is a private residence, so please be respectful. Meanwhile, the local Hibbing Library has a collection of Bob Dylan artifacts on display for visitors to stop and see when passing through town.

2425 7TH AVE. E. HIBBING. MN 55746

TRIVIA

Q **A YOUNG BOB DYLAN PROPOSED MARRIAGE TO THIS FAMOUS R&B/GOSPEL SINGER.**

Answer **MAVIS STAPLES (OF THE STAPLE SINGERS)**

Michael Jackson

As a child, Michael Jackson lived in this small house along with 10 other relatives in Gary, Indiana. Sadly, the neighborhood has seen better days and there are no options to go inside. The family lived here until 1967 when the Jackson 5 began to have success as a singing group.

2300 JACKSON AVE., GARY, IN 46407

Aretha Franklin

Aretha Franklin lived as a child here in the Memphis neighborhood known as Soulsville. The neighborhood was once home to the Stax Recording studio where artists like Sam and Dave, Al Green, and Issac Hayes recorded hit songs. Franklin died in 2018 on August 16th, the same date that another famous Memphian—Elvis Presley—met his demise. The home has a historic marker out front but doesn't offer tours.

406 LUCY AVE., MEMPHIS, TN 38106

Marlon Brando

Actor Marlon Brando was born in Omaha, Nebraska, and lived in this home from 1924–1930. Brando grew up to become a celebrated actor with roles in films like *The Godfather* and *A Streetcar Named Desire*. The house is a private residence, so please be respectful.

1026 S 32ND ST., OMAHA, NE 68105

TRIVIA

Q MARLON BRANDO ONCE DESCRIBED THIS 70S HEARTTHROB AS THE "EPITOME OF SOMETHING THAT MAKES ME WANT TO THROW UP."

Answer **BURT REYNOLDS** ★ ★ ★ ★ ★ ★

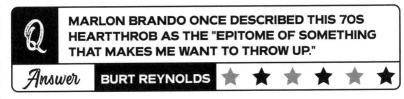

The Allman Brothers

The Allman Brothers and various relatives and friends called The Big House home from 1970–1973. In 2009, the property was renovated and turned into The Allman Brothers Band Museum. Visitors can walk through each room of the house and see original artifacts belonging to the band members along with other interesting exhibits.

"THE BIG HOUSE"
2321 VINEVILLE AVE., MACON, GA 31204
THEBIGHOUSEMUSEUM.COM

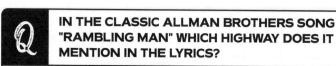

TRIVIA

Q IN THE CLASSIC ALLMAN BROTHERS SONG "RAMBLING MAN" WHICH HIGHWAY DOES IT MENTION IN THE LYRICS?

Answer HIGHWAY 41 ★ ★ ★ ★ ★ ★ ★

Bruce Springsteen

Bruce Springsteen lived in this two-family house with his parents and sister from the age of six before moving again during his high school years. If you're looking at the front of the house, the Springsteen family lived on the left side from 1955–1962.

39 ½ INSTITUTE ST., FREEHOLD, NJ 07728

Helen Keller

In 1880, Helen Keller was born in this house, known as Ivy Green, located in Tuscumbia, Alabama. Keller was an author, political activist, and the first deaf-blind person to earn a Bachelor of Arts degree. The house is now a museum in her honor and open for tours.

IVY GREEN / HELEN KELLER BIRTHPLACE MUSEUM
300 N COMMONS ST., TUSCUMBIA, AL 35674

TRIVIA

Q HELEN KELLER WAS GREAT FRIENDS WITH THIS ICONIC AMERICAN AUTHOR. THOUGH SHE WAS BLIND AND DEAF, SHE COULD TELL WHEN HE WAS NEAR BECAUSE OF HIS "DISTINCTIVE TOBACCO SCENT."

Answer MARK TWAIN—HE SMOKED 10 TO 20 CIGARS A DAY!

John F. Kennedy

John F. Kennedy was born and raised in this two-story home in Brookline, Massachusetts. The house is open for tours and operated by the National Park Service. Kennedy is one of four US presidents who were born in Norfolk County.

JOHN F. KENNEDY BIRTHPLACE NATIONAL HISTORIC SITE
83 BEALS ST., BROOKLINE, MA 02446
NPS.GOV/JOFI

Q WHO WERE THE OTHER THREE US PRESIDENTS WHO WERE BORN IN NORFOLK COUNTY, MASSACHUSETTS?

Answer JOHN ADAMS, JOHN QUINCY ADAMS, AND GEORGE H.W. BUSH

Jennifer Lopez

Jennifer Lopez grew up in the Bronx, a borough of New York City. She lived in this house along with her parents and two sisters. Her working-class parents had saved enough money to purchase the two-story home in the early 1970s. While living here, Lopez took singing and dancing lessons and regularly performed in the house for her family. This is a private residence, please be respectful.

2210 BLACKROCK AVE., BRONX, NY 10472

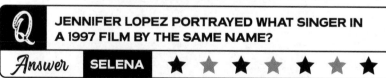

Jimmy Fallon

Jimmy Fallon became host of NBC's *The Tonight Show* in 2014. He grew up in this home in Saugerties, New York. The house went up for sale in 2012 which prompted Fallon to tweet: "Please someone cool buy it! Great place to grow up." Fallon continued to visit his parents here during weeks off from taping *Saturday Night Live*. This is a private residence, please be respectful.

102 OVERBAUGH ST., SAUGERTIES, NY 12477

TRIVIA

Q WHAT IS THE NAME OF JIMMY'S HOUSE BAND ON *THE TONIGHT SHOW*?

Answer **THE ROOTS** ★ ★ ★ ★ ★ ★ ★

Taylor Swift

Taylor Swift lived in this house for 10 years before moving to Nashville at the age of 14. The house is located in Reading, Pennsylvania, and sold in 2013 for $700,000. Swift's family also operated a nearby 11-acre Christmas tree farm when she was growing up. This is a private residence, please be respectful.

78 GRANDVIEW BLVD., READING, PA 19609

TRIVIA

Q TAYLOR SWIFT'S FIRST HIT SONG IN 2006 WAS TITLED AFTER WHAT COUNTRY MUSIC STAR?

Answer **TIM McGRAW** ★ ★ ★ ★ ★ ★

194 FINDING THE AMERICAN DREAM

INDEX

The original bread slicing machine on display in
Chillicothe, Missouri (page 172)